DAVID KALSTONE received his education at Harvard University and has taught there in the Department of English. He is now with the Department of English at Rutgers University. He is editor, with Reuben A. Brower and Anne D. Ferry, of *Beginning With Poems* (Norton).

DAVID KALSTONE

SIDNEY'S POETRY

CONTEXTS AND INTERPRETATIONS

The Norton Library
W · W · NORTON & COMPANY · INC ·
NEW YORK

SBN 393-00516-X

PUBLISHED SIMULTANEOUSLY IN CANADA
BY GEORGE J. MCLEOD LIMITED, TORONTO

PRINTED IN THE UNITED STATES OF AMERICA

1 2 3 4 5 6 7 8 9 0

50328

TO MY MOTHER AND FATHER

PREFACE

Sɪᴅɴᴇʏ's ᴄᴏɴᴄᴇʀɴ for literary tradition is evident in all his writing; so is his scorn for *mere* imitation, for the dead hand of the past in the work of those who "caught up certaine swelling phrases, which hang together, like a man which once told mee, the winde was at North West, and by South, because he would be sure to name windes enowe." This may be taken as a warning for critics as well as for poets. The interpreter of Sidney's verse must in his own reading strike a balance between a concern for background and a recognition that it takes us only so far in the confrontation of individual poems. In Sidney's case, context presents a special problem because the Italian influence on English literature has not been as enduring, as persistent, as the influence of the Greek and Latin classics. Though the Italian background is by no means the only one relevant to the *Arcadia* or to *Astrophel and Stella*, it is now one of the least familiar. We do not read Petrarch as often as we should; we certainly never read Sannazaro. This study is partly devoted to recovering strains of the Italian literary past that would have had lively importance for Sidney as a poet. I should add that the "contexts" of my title are not only those of a tradition, but also those provided by a writer's total work. I have brought to bear upon the understanding of Sidney's poems a great deal of his prose, par-

PREFACE

ticularly that of the *Arcadia*. My purpose throughout is to
suggest a framework within which Sidney's verse may be
read and an approach to lyrics whose richer effects might
otherwise escape us.

* * *

It was the late Rosemond Tuve, with her learned regard
for Sidney, who first taught me to value his poetry and helped
me to undertake this study.

At Harvard I have benefited from the generous criticism
and encouragement of Professors Harry Levin and Reuben
Brower, who read this work in an early form, and from the
kind advice of Professors Herschel Baker and Douglas Bush.
William Abrahams, Tom Cole, Professor Dante Della Terza,
Anne Davidson Ferry, and Neil Rudenstine have helped me
with the manuscript in important ways, as has Joyce Lebo-
witz of Harvard University Press. For their continuing interest and for all their suggestions, I bear a special obligation
to Professors Paul J. Alpers and Stephen Orgel.

Anyone who writes about Sidney stands in the debt of
William A. Ringler, Jr., who has established a secure text in
The Poems of Sir Philip Sidney. To Oxford University Press
I owe thanks for permission to quote from it. Cambridge Uni-
versity Press has kindly granted me permission to include
passages from *The Prose Works of Sir Philip Sidney*.

A word about the Italian quotations: I have thought it important to leave them in the original and have supplied prose
translations of my own as literal aids.

Lowell House   D. K.
Cambridge, Massachusetts
1 January 1965

CONTENTS

TEXTS AND ABBREVIATIONS

All citations of Sidney's verse are from *The Poems of Sir Philip Sidney*, ed. William A. Ringler, Jr. (Oxford: Clarendon Press, 1962). Poems are identified by the following abbreviations and the number assigned them in Ringler's edition:

Arc.	*The Countesse of Pembroke's Arcadia*
AS	*Astrophel and Stella*
CS	*Certaine Sonets*
LM	*The Lady of May*

I depart from the Oxford text in keeping the more familiar "Astrophel" rather than adopting the editor's restoration of "Astrophil." As Ringler points out (p. 458), Sidney provided no title for his work, and there is sixteenth-century authority for either usage. I have also followed a uniform typography for the sonnets, in the manner of the 1598 folio, rather than varying the indentations with the rhyme scheme. (For the advantages and authority of the latter patterning, see Ringler, p. 448.)

Citations from Sidney's prose are identified by the following abbreviation with the appropriate volume and page appended:

F   *The Complete Works of Sir Philip Sidney*, ed. Albert Feuillerat, 4 vols. (Cambridge, Eng.: Cambridge University Press, 1912–1926).

In all quotations, peculiarities of Elizabethan typography, principally in the use of *u* and *v*, are made to conform to modern usage.

SIDNEY'S POETRY

CONTEXTS AND INTERPRETATIONS

INTRODUCTION

Here's Pastor Fido . . .
. . . All our English writers,
I mean such as are happy in the Italian,
Will deign to steal out of this author, mainly,
Almost as much as from Montagnié:
He has so modern, and facile a vein,
Fitting the time, and catching the court-ear.
Your Petrarch is more passionate, yet he,
In days of sonneting, trusted 'em with much:
Dante is hard, and few can understand him.
Volpone, III.iv.86–95

LADY POLITIC Would-Be's observation is true as far as it goes: an interest in the literature of the Italian Renaissance was important for English poets and poetasters alike. But the quality or the significance of their interest — these are not considerations with which we would expect her to be concerned. They are, however, problems for the critic. It is easy enough to identify individual lines cribbed by English poetasters from their Italian models. It is also easy to see how the giants of Italian poetry serve as ideal figures to be invoked, the masters of their genres; Spenser is said to have announced *The Faerie Queene* as an effort to "overgo Ariosto," and Harington paid tribute to Sir Philip Sidney as an "English Petrarke." [1] Still, Sidney's Astrophel is probably remembered by most readers of *Astrophel and Stella* for his mockery of those who "search for everie purling spring, /

[1]

Which from the ribs of old *Parnassus* flowes . . . / You that poore *Petrarch's* long deceased woes, / With new-borne sighes and denisend wit do sing." The critical tone is characteristic, warning readers against easy assumptions about the relation of Sidney's sonnet sequence to its Italian parent, the *Canzoniere* of Petrarch, and the host of French and Italian Petrarchans. Modern scholars have listed enough borrowings from Petrarch and the Petrarchans to qualify our sense of Sidney's independence. But his relation to those predecessors is not something that can be defined mechanically by counting debts or by fixing him with our commonplace terms, Petrarchan and anti-Petrarchan. It is one of the curious facts of his literary biography that Sidney, if he marks the beginning of the vogue for sonnet cycles in England, marks almost the end of a highly sophisticated tradition in Europe. Praised by contemporaries as the English Petrarch, he shows ironic regard for a tradition, Italian and French, of which he is one of the last representatives. It is his energetic awareness of this position that sets him apart. In his sonnets, he both participates in and questions "poore Petrarch's long deceased woes"; he revitalizes the Petrarchan vision while calling its values into question.

Sidney's self-consciousness was one way of reacting to a problem that was general in English Renaissance poetry, the problem of domesticating several centuries of European literary experience. In addition to differences of time and place, historical circumstance and individual temperament, English writers had to face the complications arising from the simple fact that their "Renaissance" in poetry came late. They are subject at once to the currents and countercurrents of Renaissance literature, the spirit of witty skepticism existing in concentrated form beside continued efforts in traditional genres. As the quotation from *Volpone* suggests, the three centuries that divide "more passionate" Petrarch from "modern and facile" Guarini or from the probing Montaigne are compressed into or, to be more accurate, press in as influences upon two decades of English verse and drama.

The study that follows is concerned with Sidney's poetry, both the pastoral verse of *The Countesse of Pembroke's Arcadia* and the love sonnets of *Astrophel and Stella*, with particular emphasis on Sidney's conception of the Italian genres. The distance from which he has fetched individual lines does not concern me as much as a larger question to which such information contributes: how far in his versions of Arcadian pastoral and the Petrarchan love sonnet has he traveled from the classical Italian notions of those genres? Or to put the problem in another way: what elements of the traditional background help us to become more appreciative readers of Sidney's poetry? in what context should we read his verse? and what qualities of his own does he bring to the conventions of Petrarchan and pastoral poetry?

In a sense, the division between pastoral verse and sonnets is a deceptive one. In both cases we are dealing with love poetry and with the development of Sidney as a love poet. To study Sidney's adaptations of Italian genres is to introduce ourselves to his sharply defined attitudes toward Petrarchan love. By comparison with the poetry of his contemporary Spenser, or with that of Shakespeare, the range of Sidney's poetry is narrow indeed. Modern readers who find pleasure in his verse will in fact not take it from the variety of "things of this world" that he includes, but rather from a quality of his awareness. Where a reader senses vivacity and intensity, he can usually discover Sidney ringing changes on continental conventions.

This study of Sidney's poetry begins with his *Arcadia*, where the problem of recovering the European perspective is particularly relevant to our appreciation. Even if one has acquired a taste for Renaissance pastoral, for its leisurely fiction, Sidney's work seems eccentric. Familiar themes — the Golden Age, the death of shepherds, the praise of country over town — are not central to his pastoral lyrics. They grow in part, these Arcadian poems so narrowly concerned with love, from an Italian mode, the pastoral verse of Sannazaro. Sannazaro's *Arcadia*, a book we no longer read, enjoyed success, respect, and above all imitation. In calling it up, as he does, Sidney is able to count upon his readers to respond with a certain fullness and to appreciate the way the poet etches his reaction to the languor of Sannazaro's golden world. As in the later *Astrophel and Stella*, he can play his poems against conventions that flourished in Italian erotic poetry. In the eclogues and occasional pastoral verse of the *Arcadia*, one can begin to recognize attitudes toward love and love poetry that emerge, transformed, in Sidney's sonnet sequence. Too often the Arcadian poems are mentioned as experimental simply because they demonstrate the interest in verse forms and meters that Sidney also displayed in his translation of *The Psalms of David*. But critics have begun to view that alert experimentation less mechanically and to see it as only one aspect of a distinctive poetic sensibility. Both William Empson and Theodore Spencer have won readers for the great double sestina "Yee Gote-heard Gods." [2] It is the best introduction to the *Arcadia* and can stand alone, attractive in its melancholy particularity. The weaker of Sidney's Arcadian poems require support from the fabric of his pastoral writing as a whole; but read in context, they emerge as part of an attempt to give dramatic shape to a singular view of pastoral retirement and the world of love.

Astrophel and Stella, of course, contains a richer vein of poetry; it is more accessible and more immediately engaging.

Yet even these poems gain in resonance when read against their Petrarchan background and in the light of the *Arcadia*. It is typical of Sidney's critical mind to weigh in that romance the heroic past of his Greek warriors against the pastoral leisure of their present experience in Arcadia. Although the heroic subject is almost entirely absent from *Astrophel and Stella*, its pressure is felt often. In the background of this sonnet sequence — and in the foreground of the first thirty or so sonnets — is the figure of the knight "who spoyles himselfe of blisse." Astrophel's responsiveness to the demands of the active life is the source of conflict earlier in the sequence and from the outset stirs him against taking Petrarchan conventions at face value. His dilemma is not unlike that of Pyrocles and Musidorus, the heroes of the *Arcadia*. Yet the flexibility of the speaker in *Astrophel and Stella* makes all the difference between his complaints and the laments of the Arcadian heroes, between the nimble surprises of the sonnet sequence and the stylized patterns of the Arcadian poems. The achievement of *Astrophel and Stella*, as we shall see, is not the discovery of a new subject or even the exploration of new attitudes, but rather Sidney's recognition of the dramatic possibilities of both the individual sonnet and the sonnet sequence. The energies released in *Astrophel and Stella* are already present in the *Arcadia*.

PART ONE

THE POETRY OF ARCADIA

1

THE TRANSFORMATION OF ARCADIA

"This," he [Don Quixote] observed, "is the meadow where we
fell in with those gallant and gaily bedecked shepherds and
shepherdesses who were endeavoring to imitate and restore the
Arcadia of old, a novel idea and an inspired one; and if you
approve, Sancho, I would suggest that, at least for the time that
I have to live in retirement, we likewise turn shepherds. . . .
Together we will roam the hills, the woods, and the meadows,
now singing songs and now composing elegies, drinking the
crystal water of the springs or that of the clear running brooks
or mighty rivers. . . . Song will be our joy, and we shall be
happy even in our laments, for Apollo will supply the inspiration for our verses and love will endow us with conceits and
we shall be everlastingly famous — not only in this age but for
all time to come."

Cervantes, *Don Quixote* (tr. Putnam), II.lxvii

THE POETIC LANDSCAPE of Arcadia was, of course, a familiar
one by the time that Sidney came to write *The Countesse of
Pembroke's Arcadia* in the late 1570s. It was Virgil who had
made Arcadia the home of the pastoral eclogue and bestowed
upon it the haunting qualities of the ideal: "luxuriant vegeta-
tion, eternal spring, and inexhaustible leisure for love." [1] But,
close at hand, the sixteenth-century poet had other visions of
Arcady, transformations and embellishments of the Arcadian

landscape that still paid tribute to the continuing effect of Virgil's eclogues upon the Renaissance imagination. Of all such metamorphoses, the *Arcadia* of Jacopo Sannazaro, published in Venice in 1502, most suited the century's taste and exercised the widest influence. This work, the first set of vernacular eclogues actually to be set in Arcadia,[2] established Sannazaro in the eyes of his contemporaries as the modern master of pastoral verse. Within a decade of the publication of his *Arcadia*, he had been given a place among the few moderns depicted in Raphael's Parnassus in the Vatican Stanze; Petrarch, Boccaccio, Ariosto, Tebaldeo, and Dante are the others. Commentaries appeared: the first in 1556, followed by two others before 1600.[3] When Sannazaro died near Naples in 1530, Bembo was able to point out, in a well-known epigram, the appropriateness of burying him near Virgil, and Cervantes, in a description of Naples from the sea, directed readers immediately to the "most famous mountain" in the world that held the ashes of the two renowned pastoral poets.[4] The Italian work set off waves of pastoral verse in Italy and Spain, in France and England, capturing the imagination of poets as different in spirit as Ronsard and Sir Philip Sidney. Sidney, considering the problem of diction in pastoral poetry, quite naturally refers his readers to *"Theocritus* in Greeke, *Virgill* in Latine, [and] *Sanazara* in Italian."[5]

Yet Sannazaro has earned his place in the literary histories through tributes and imitations rather than through a continuing appreciation of his verse. His incontestable appeal to his contemporaries requires some explanation. We may begin with his sixteenth-century French translator, Jean Martin, who presents the Italian Arcadia with a flourish to "gentilz hommes et dames vivans noblement en leurs mesnages aux champz," gentlemen and ladies living nobly in their retreats in the fields:

elle [ceste Arcadie] ne represente que Nymphes gracieuses, et jolyes bergeres, pour l'amour desquelles, jeunes pasteurs soubz le frais umbrage des petiz arbrisseaux et entre les murmures des fontaines chantent plusieurs belles chansons, industrieusement tirees des divins Poetes Theocrite et Virgile: avec lesquelles s'accorde melodieusement le ramage des oysillons degoysans sus les branches verdes, tellement que les escoutans pensent estre raviz aux champs Elysées.[6]

Martin conveys exactly the refinement that classical pastoral has undergone in Sannazaro; in this courtly framework one does not encounter the rough bucolic detail to be found in Theocritus and often in Virgil. The Italian *Arcadia*, from Martin's description, emerges as a hybrid work. Echoes of Theocritus and Virgil take their place in "belles chansons" meant for the ears of graceful nymphs and shepherdesses; the songs harmonize with the murmur of fountains and the singing of birds. It is a sketch for Watteau. To a twentieth-century reader, Sannazaro sounds anything but classical; his echoes of Virgil seem as romantic as Keats's do of Spenser.

Martin, in his account, speaks of eclogues as if they were primarily love songs, a fact that goes far to explain the appeal of Sannazaro. In the Venetian edition of the *Arcadia* (1502), the printer's preface refers to its poems as "canzone et aegloghe," thereby declaring their double ancestry.[7] It is not simply that some of the familiar classical singing contests and shepherds' dialogues are cast in the form of the canzone. (Of the twelve eclogues of the *Arcadia*, two indeed are Petrarchan canzoni and two are sestine in the strict form descending from Provençal poetry into Italian verse.) More important, the entire *Arcadia* is shot through with the developed cadences and conventions of Petrarchan poetry, and its landscape echoes with the complaints of unhappy lovers.

Don Quixote is able to take the heightened role of love for

granted when he proposes to Sancho that they imitate the Arcadians of old: "for Apollo will supply the inspiration for our verses and love will endow us with conceits and we shall be everlastingly famous." It is not surprising, of course, to find love in the pastoral world. As Curtius remarks, pastoral "for two millenniums . . . draws to itself the majority of erotic motifs." [8] But it does indicate a shift in emphasis, a concentration of interest, to find Amor beside Apollo as one of the tutelary deities of poetic inspiration. More is being recognized than the pleasures and pains of love among shepherds; that concern is beautifully rendered in Theocritus. To say that "love will endow us with conceits and we shall be everlastingly famous" promises some precise and vital connection between love and the poetic imagination, between pastoral love poetry and poetic fame. It is just that connection, richly suggested by Petrarch, which Sannazaro's *Arcadia* makes explicit again and again.

What follows here is not a full-scale analysis of Sannazaro's *Arcadia*, but rather an attempt to see what he contributed to the transformation of Virgil's Arcady. In the strict sense Sannazaro was a source — one of several — for the English *Arcadia*; the references are important though not frequent. But even where Sidney does not depend on verbal allusion to Sannazaro, he implies by echoing the setting and title of a book so famous that he writes against a well-defined and familiar background, a coherent version of pastoral. To describe Sannazaro's version and its roots is to recapture some sense of what meanings Arcadia had accumulated by the sixteenth century. The Italian was able to present it as an archetype of perfect bliss, a paradise for poets, and at the same time as a refuge for the complaining lover of Petrarchan poetry. To older visions of a golden world he accommodated a newer dramatic figure in a landscape and a different way of seeing the lover's distress symbolized in pastoral verse. Despite its perfectly harmonized surface, Sannazaro's work is an ambitious, at times uneasy, wedding of traditions. What Sidney learned from it and what he reacted against will be part of my subject.

1

The poems of Sannazaro's *Arcadia* are almost all laments: laments for the dead, laments for the passing of the Golden Age, but primarily lovers' laments. When Sannazaro bids a prose farewell to the *sampogna*, the shepherd's bagpipe, he remembers it as the instrument "insegnando le rispondenti selve di risonare il nome de la tua donna" (teaching the responding woods to resound with the name of your lady).[9] Here he imitates a pastoral pleasure of Virgil's Tityrus: "Formosam resonare doces Amaryllida silvas," teaching the woods to re-echo "fair Amaryllis." [10] But Sannazaro goes on to characterize the lover's song more closely: "E se mai pastore alcuno per sorte in cose liete adoprar ti volesse; fagli prima intendere, che tu non sai se non piangere e lamentarti" (And if ever some shepherd by chance wishes to use you in happy matters, have him first understand that you know nothing, if not to weep and to lament).[11] The *sampogna* knows only how to lament. It is characteristic of the Italian tradition and of Sannazaro that thoughts of love should be tinged with melancholy (whether, as in this instance, over the death of his mistress or, in others, over his unfulfilled love).

The experience being dramatized in these Italian poems differs radically from that of the love complaints to be found in Virgilian pastoral. Even in Virgil's tenth eclogue, which seems most like Sannazaro, centering as it does on a complaining lover who has come to Arcadia for consolation, the speaker assumes that love would be simpler in the pastoral world:

"hic gelidi fontes, hic mollia prata, Lycori, / hic nemus; hic
ipso tecum consumerer aevo" (here are cold springs, Lycoris,
here soft meadows, here woodland; here, with thee, time alone
would wear me away — *Ecl.* X.42–43). With no enemy but
devouring time, the pastoral scene is, in the words of a later
Latin poet, *dignus amore locus*, a place fit for love.[12] The
attitude holds implicitly a wish that is best rendered in English poetry by Marlowe's well-known pastoral invitation:

> Come live with me, and be my Love,
> And we will all the pleasures prove,
> That Vallies, Groves, hills and fields,
> Woods, or steepie mountaines yeeldes.

Lovers in Sannazaro's *Arcadia* do not generally see the
possibility of happiness in their pastoral retirement. The
tone is set by Sincero, the figure who gives the work what
unity it has. In the seventh prose episode he describes himself as an exile from Naples who has come to Arcadia to escape
the suffering of the courtly lover; he of course does not escape, and his accents echo those of the complaining shepherds
in the Arcadian eclogues:

> Niuna fiera, nè ucello, nè ramo vi sento movere, ch'io non mi
> gire paventoso per mirare se fusse dessa in queste parti venuta
> ad intendere la misera vita, ch'io sostegno per lei: similmente
> niuna altra cosa vedere vi posso, che prima non mi sia cagione
> di rimembrarmi con più fervore e sollicitudine di lei; e mi pare
> che le concave grotte, i fonti, le valli, i monti, con tutte le
> selve la chiamino, e gli alti arbusti risoneno sempre il nome di
> lei.*   (*Opere*, p. 111)

---

* No wild beast, nor bird, nor branch do I hear move, without turning,
fearful, to see whether she herself might have come into these parts to hear
of the miserable life I bear for her sake; similarly I can see no other thing
there, without its first being the cause that reminds me, with more fervor
and care, of her; and it seems to me that the hollow caves, the springs, the
valleys, the mountains, along with all the woods, call her, and the high trees
resound continually with her name.

We are in the presence of a familiar dramatic figure. This unhappy lover in retreat who finds signs of his state in every bird and every branch, in valleys and mountains, is to be found often in Renaissance canzoni and above all in the poetry of Petrarch:

> I' l'ho più volte (or chi fia che m'il creda?)
> ne l'acqua chiara e sopra l'erba verde
> veduto viva, e nel troncon d'un faggio,
> e'n bianca nube sì fatta che Leda
> avria ben detto che sua figlia perde,
> come stella che'l sol copre col raggio.*

What marks both Italian passages off from the brief examples I have quoted from Virgil and Marlowe is a different symbolic use of the details of landscape. Virgil's lines seem direct: the details — fountains, meadows, woods — combined with direct address to his faithless mistress suggest a richness in pastoral love if she will only join him. The assumption of the complaint is that she will not, but he does project an image of possible fullness in love. By contrast the mood of the Petrarch and Sannazaro passages is retrospective and nostalgic. They imply no gesture of invitation, and the details of fountains, meadows, and woods are not presented as settings for love but rather as springs for the memory. The poet is necessarily, and in a sense happily, alone. Pastoral beauty suggests to his imagination the beauty of his mistress and its corollary, her unattainability; he ponders constantly her absence and its extreme form, her death. The landscape is

* I have often seen her vividly (now who is there who will believe me?) in clear water and on the green grass and in the trunk of a beech, and in a white cloud so made that Leda would indeed have said that her daughter [Helen] was surpassed, like a star that the sun conceals with its rays. [Francesco Petrarca, *Rime e Trionfi*, ed. Raffaello Ramat (Milan, 1957), number 129, lines 40–45. Citations from Petrarch are all from this edition. The first number is that of the poem in most modern editions; the second set is line numbers.]

almost exclusively and abstractly connected with meditation, with invention. This association between pastoral wandering and thinking about love is explicit in the opening lines of the canzone from which I have just quoted:

> Di pensier in pensier, di monte in monte
>> mi guida Amor, ch'ogni segnato calle
>> provo contrario a la tranquilla vita.*

(Rime, 129)

Petrarch may be termed the *locus classicus* for this familiar dramatic figure and voice. His governing influence in Italian poetry is responsible for the difference that a reader immediately senses between a Virgilian eclogue and the graceful laments of Sincero in the Italian *Arcadia*. In view of the extent to which Sannazaro was influenced by Petrarch and borrowed from him, it is worthwhile to define certain features of the Petrarchan style. The instructive comparison between him and Sannazaro is to be made in the ways in which each poet uses pastoral retirement as a dramatic situation to give point and precision to the love complaint.

We may take the following sonnet of Petrarch as a beginning:

> Pien di quella ineffabile dolcezza
>> che del bel viso trassen gli occhi miei
>> nel dì che volentier chiusi gli avrei
>> per non mirar già mai minor bellezza,
> lassai quel ch'i' più bramo; et ho sì avezza
>> la mente a contemplar sola costei,
>> ch'altro non vede, e ciò che non è lei
>> già per antica usanza odia e disprezza.
> In una valle chiusa d'ogn'intorno
>> ch'è refrigerio de' sospir miei lassi,
>> giunsi sol con Amor, pensoso e tardo.

* From thought to thought, from mountain to mountain, love guides me, since I find every marked path hostile to a tranquil life.

Ivi non donne, ma fontane e sassi,
e l'imagine trovo di quel giorno
che'l pensier mio figura, ovunque io sguardo.*

(*Rime*, 116)

Petrarch is not a varied poet; to touch the *Canzoniere* at any point is to introduce oneself to the paradoxes that characterize the inevitable separation of poet from mistress. In the sonnet above, the poet is undertaking a version of the *vita nuova*, the lover's new life; his metaphor for that experience is movement into the pastoral world. The poem holds in solution contrary emotions: on one hand the "ineffabile dolcezza," the sweetness he drew from seeing Laura, and, on the other hand, the "sospir lassi," the unhappy sighs of exile. What binds these contrary feelings together and gives them psychological force is the rightness of tone by which Petrarch suggests that one experience evokes the other. The poem moves from the wonder and appreciation with which he first saw Laura ("pien di quella ineffabile dolcezza") to a willingness to close his eyes and see no lesser beauty. The physical exile that follows enacts just the experience of that muted hyperbole. Without any explanation and with a tone of knowing acceptance, he leaves her. With the scene of the enclosed valley ("una valle chiusa") and its recall of the phrase "chiusi gli avrei," he emphasizes the change that has taken place: the closing of the physical eyes ("ch'altro non vede") and the concentration on vision in the mind's eye ("et ho sì avezza / la mente a contemplar sola costei").

* Full of that indescribable sweetness which my eyes drew from that lovely face on the day when I would freely have closed them so as never to look on a lesser beauty, I left what I most desire; and I so accustomed my mind to contemplate only her that it sees nothing else, and what is not hers I already hate and scorn as an old habit. In a valley enclosed all around, which is solace for my weary sighs, I have arrived alone with Love, pensive and slow. Here I find no women — rather springs and stones and the image of that day which my thought shapes for me, wherever I look.

In his mind, then, he associates the enclosed valley, its fountains and stones, with the memory of Laura's face. The poem is informed by the strength of that first vision — it absorbs all his inventive powers. Imagination inevitably separates him from society, which has become unimportant to him, and from Laura, whose perfection inspires not only desire but awe and fear. The experience enriches and exhausts the poet; it accounts both for the splendid scorn of "ciò che non è lei / già per antica usanza odia e disprezza" and for the languor of "pensoso e tardo." In the appropriate figure of the "valle chiusa" (with its punning reference to Petrarch's own seclusion at Vaucluse) he embodies the whole notion of pastoral exile and isolation, where the initial vision can, in recollection, be painfully and perfectly maintained. The complaints of Sannazaro's shepherds are to resound in this symbolic valley, and it is to provide the scene for Strephon and Klaius, who sing the double sestina in Sidney's *Arcadia*.

The pastoral wanderer appears and reappears as a dramatic figure in the *Canzoniere*. The same words echo throughout the poems of exile (words like *pensoso, sospiri, dolcezza, affanno*). Variations, when they occur, are subtle rather than spectacular — modulations in half tones, which must prove the despair of Petrarch's translators. There are, for example, many less satisfying resolutions than the close of "Pien di quella ineffabile dolcezza." The isolation, pensiveness, and heightened vision of love are combined in the context of a more restless pastoral exile (to choose only one instance) in the sonnet that opens

> Solo e pensoso i più deserti campi
> vo mesurando a passi tardi e lenti,
> e gli occhi porto per fuggire intenti,
> ove vestigio uman l'arena stampi.*

(*Rime,* 35)

* Alone and thoughtful, I go pacing the most deserted fields with

It closes, as does "Pien di quella ineffabile dolcezza," with Amor as the poet's companion:

> Ma pur sì aspre vie, né sì selvagge
>   cercar non so ch'Amor non venga sempre
>   ragionando con meco; et io con lui.*

But here the note of conclusion is more disturbed. The vision of love does not console or satisfy; it simply haunts. It can not be exorcised or reasoned away. The poet stresses flight, and less richness, less of "ineffabile dolcezza," rewards his retirement.

In the more ambitious "Di pensier in pensier," one of his most beautiful canzone, Petrarch returns to the contrasting possibilities of landscape, its bleakness and its richness for the lover. The canzone form, with greater freedom than is possible in a single sonnet, allows him to register a complicated movement of thought and feeling. "Di pensier in pensier" traces the intricate process of remembering and imagining Laura. It oscillates between the poet's despair and the growing intensity with which he grasps Laura's beauty in his thoughts. Each turn of feeling is marked as a stage in his restless wandering to seek out the high mountains and wild woods ("ogni abitato loco / è nemico mortal degli occhi miei"). After frequent shifts, the poem culminates in a stanza that renders the extremes of feeling as inseparable:

> I' l'ho più volte (or chi fia che m'il creda?)
>   ne l'acqua chiara e sopra l'erba verde
>   veduto viva, e nel troncon d'un faggio,
>   e'n bianca nube sì fatta che Leda
>   avria ben detto che sua figlia perde,
>   come stella che 'l sol copre col raggio;

---

lingering, slow steps, and I watch intently to flee from places where human traces mark the sand.

* But yet I am not able to seek out any paths so harsh or so wild, that Love does not always come along discoursing with me; and I with him.

[19]

    e quanto in più selvaggio
    loco mi trovo e 'n più deserto lido,
    tanto più bella il mio pensier l'adombra.
    Poi quando il vero sgombra
    quel dolce error, pur lì medesmo assido
    me freddo, pietra morta, in pietra viva,
    in guisa d'uom che pensi e pianga e scriva.*

                                        (*Rime*, 129:40–52)

Poetic interest in the passage centers on the brilliance of
the poet's pastoral vision of Laura and on the bleakness of
his own state while imagining her beauty. Petrarch renders
both states through a choice of pastoral detail toward which
he has been building carefully through the earlier sections
of the poem. He graces a remembered image of her by discovering it in clear waters and green meadows and in the
whiteness of a cloud more beautiful than Helen. Juxtaposed
with that vision are lines in which he sees himself as cold as
stone, "pietra morta." But Petrarch depends on more than
simple symbolic associations of pastoral richness with Laura
and barrenness with her lover. The details are woven into a
fully imagined dramatic situation. As in the sonnets, pastoral
exile is a world for poetic meditation ("di pensier in pensier,
di monte in monte"). Early in the poem, wanderings of the
mind beguile the wandering lover: "A ciascun passo nasce un
penser novo / de la mia donna." In a more welcoming landscape ("Ove porge ombra un pino alto od un colle / talor
m'arresto") a memory of Laura's face ("e pur nel primo sasso
/ disegno co la mente il suo bel viso") replaces thoughts of

* I have often seen her vividly (now who is there who will believe me?)
in clear water and on the green grass and in the trunk of a beech, and in a
white cloud so made that Leda would indeed have said that her daughter
was surpassed, like a star that the sun conceals with its rays; and the more
savage the place and more deserted the shore where I find myself, the more
beautiful my thought shadows her forth. Then when truth clears away that
sweet error, I still sit there the same — cold, dead stone on living stone, the
semblance of a man who thinks and weeps and writes.

her aloofness. The vocabulary he uses to describe such moments of vision is significant: in this stanza, *disegno* (draw); in the climactic stanza of the poem, *adombra* (shadow forth or, technically, to shade a drawing). In sonnet 116 (discussed above) he discovers among springs and stones "l'imagine . . . che'l pensier mio figura." In another canzone, he gazes at her face "per *inscolpirlo* imaginando in parte / onde mai né per forza né per arte / mosso sarà," to carve her image where neither force nor deception might remove it (*Rime*, 50:66–68). The verbs in each case are associated with the visual or plastic arts, and the actor is the poet's mind, *la mente*, or thought, *il pensier*. The brief, brilliant moments of pastoral happiness measure not merely Laura's beauty, but also the richness of pictorial imagination that her beauty inspires in him. This, rather than any promise of her favors, is the satisfactory experience.

The climactic stanza of "Di pensier in pensier" makes a further statement about the poet-lover's experience: the imagination becomes purer and fiercer as he gets further from society and from his mistress:

> e quanto in più selvaggio
> loco mi trovo e'n più deserto lido,
> tanto più bella il mio pensier l'adombra.

But entwined with this visionary moment is the perception that illusion has its price; it does not dispel for long the pains of physical separation. When truth destroys his vision ("quel dolce error"), he becomes cold, the semblance of a man who thinks and weeps and writes. At the end of the stanza with its reminder of the poem that is being written, even the act of imagining takes on by juxtaposition with "pietra morta" the lifelessness of the deprived lover. We have moved in this stanza from a wondrous opening to a bleak close and in the process experienced an unavoidable tension between the role of poet and the role of lover.

Although I have given only a small sample of the handling of this pastoral theme in the *Rime*, these few details are enough to suggest something of Petrarch's special qualities. The dramatic situation of the lover in a landscape is one of the sirens of European literature, and its call was an energizing one for many poets, including Sidney and Sannazaro. The wailing shepherds of minor Renaissance poetry often convey to a reader little more than self-pity as they call for consolation in forests and meadows, beside fountains and streams. The Petrarchan lover escapes self-pity because for him the pastoral setting is part of a serious statement about memory and imagination in their relation to love. Although he does not regard pastoral abundance as an invitation to physical love ("Come live with me, and be my Love"), he identifies it with a fullness of invention, part of the new life that love brings to the poet. From this feeling springs the pun "Laura–lauro" — the latter meaning both laurel tree and poetic laurel — that seems so bald if one comes upon it undramatized and unadorned in the *Rime*; his love for Laura is reflected in Nature's abundance, the flourishing laurel, and in his own poetic fame. "Love will endow us with conceits," Don Quixote is to announce to Sancho Panza in praising the pastoral life.

But Petrarch always takes care to remind his readers of pastoral bleakness, which conveys the other side of the experience, the pains of self-imposed exile. The perfection that Laura embodies and that makes her his Muse does, as it did for Dante and the poets of the *dolce stil nuovo*, separate him from his mistress. Petrarch, constantly balancing the roles of poet and lover against each other, sees them as inescapable contraries of a single experience. The Petrarchan opposites, the vision of love as "dolce amaro," sweet and bitter, are the easiest element in his style to imitate, so that the oxymoron became the staple of centuries of Petrarchan poetry. But very few of his imitators approached the skill with which Petrarch himself created the convincing and accurate dramatic situations that give point to his paradoxes. Petrarch at his best represents standards of precision in the use of pastoral detail in love poetry that are valuable in judging all his successors — Sannazaro among them.

2

Sincero, the central figure of Sannazaro's *Arcadia,* is another lover in retreat. But the landscape into which he wanders is not desolate or marked by solitude. Sincero's complaints are mirrored in the eclogues of the shepherds of Arcadia, who sing in the manner we have seen characterized by Martin: "jeunes pasteurs . . . entre les murmures des fontaines chantent plusieurs belles chansons, industrieusement tirees des divins Poetes Theocrite et Virgile: avec lesquelles s'accorde melodieusement le ramage des oysillons." A landscape that echoes with the great pastoral verse of the ancients consoles and moderates the laments of the unhappy lover; harmony informs Sannazaro's verse beyond the Petrarchan measure. What appears to be happening in Sannazaro is a conflation of the Virgilian pastoral poet, the shepherd of Arcady, with the Petrarchan poet-lover, in exile in the pastoral world. The framework, the Virgilian setting with its shepherds who are masters of song, makes an enormous difference, providing a tempting shift of poetic focus. Though lovers complain, Sannazaro's governing response appears to be "i sospiri si convertirono in dolce suono" — sighs transform themselves into sweet sound (*Opere,* p. 153). A major critical question emerges: what effect has such an attitude upon the delicate balance that Petrarch's verse maintains between a delight in pastoral richness and imagination, on one hand, and the pains of separation from his mistress, on the other.

The structure of Sannazaro's *Arcadia* is deceptive. At first glance it appears to be a prose narrative with interspersed poems, modeled after the *Vita Nuova* of Dante and the *Ameto* of Boccaccio. Actually Sannazaro's prose does not carry a continuous narrative as the earlier Italian works do. The twelve prose episodes are free-standing pieces, only loosely connected with one another by their Arcadian setting and by the reappearance of Sincero. They encase Sannazaro's eclogues, which are independent poems, a series of "selected pieces" in the Virgilian manner, and they explain the circumstances in which each eclogue is sung. The *Arcadia*, in effect, moves from one gathering of shepherds to another through an atmosphere haunted by the sound of the *sampogna*.

Yet the proses should not be dismissed as mere transitions. At least one of them is a full-scale prose version of a neo-Latin pastoral poem, an elegy of Nemesian. Others are descriptive, representing an expansion of the kind of detail with which Virgil introduced some of his eclogues. A comparison with the economical use of pastoral detail in Virgil is instructive. Sometimes Virgil marks his settings simply as invitations to shade and song:

> Cur non, Mopse, boni quoniam convenimus ambo,
> tu calamos inflare levis, ego dicere versus,
> hic corylis mixtas inter consedimus ulmos?*
>
> (*Ecl.* V.1–3)

In the fourth eclogue, he uses pastoral detail as an index of

*Mopsus, now that we have met, good men both, you at breathing in slender reeds, I at singing verses — why not seat ourselves among these elms, with hazels interspersed?

[24]

perfection and a coming Golden Age. Often he invokes it to suggest the elegiac consolations of twilight and pastoral simplicity:

> Hic tamen hanc mecum poteras requiescere noctem
> fronde super viridi: sunt nobis mitia poma,
> castaneae molles et pressi copia lactis;
> et iam summa procul villarum culmina fumant
> maioresque cadunt altis de montibus umbrae.*
>
> (*Ecl.* I.79–83)

But Sannazaro magnifies the role of setting. "Atmosphere" assumes enormous importance and draws attention to itself almost with the force of independent lyric poems. As Curtius remarks, "In Theocritus and Virgil such scenes are merely backgrounds for the ensuing pastoral poetry. But they were soon detached from any larger context and became subjects of bravura rhetorical description." [13]

Naturally the mood of the proses affects the texture of verse in the eclogues. Sannazaro's second eclogue, for instance, ends in a singing contest between two shepherds, Uranio and Montano, each complaining of the cruelty of a shepherdess. The poem furnishes a drastic example of the fate of Petrarchan material in this *Arcadia*. Sannazaro expends a great deal of ingenuity in varying the stanzas with which the lovers challenge one another,[14] but the conceits merely echo the familiar Petrarchan opposites. The lover's sweet torments and his simultaneous freezing and burning are employed without any of the careful dramatic justification they receive in the best of Petrarch's poems. Then in the closing stanzas of the eclogue, as the two singers invoke twilight, the poetic

---

* Yet this night you might have rested here with me on the green leafage. We have ripe apples, mealy chestnuts, and a wealth of pressed cheeses. Even now the house-tops yonder send up smoke and longer shadows fall from the mountain-heights.

atmosphere thickens. Pain is dissolved into elegiac sentiment and hushed appreciation of scene and song. The muted close of Virgil's first eclogue accounts for the mood and even for some of the details.[15] But characteristically Sannazaro, while responding to the mood of his source, diffuses the Virgilian energy. His lingering sixteen-line conclusion serves the function of Virgil's five lines:

> MONTANO: Ecco la notte; e'l ciel tutto s'imbruna,
>   e gli alti monti le contrade adombrano;
>   le stelle n'accompagnano e la luna.
> E le mie pecorelle il bosco sgombrano
>   inseme ragunate, che ben sanno
>   il tempo e l'ora che la mandra ingombrano.
> Andiamo appresso, noi: chè lor sen vanno,
>   Uranio mio; e già i compagni aspettano,
>   e forse temen di successo danno.
> URANIO: Montano, i miei compagni non suspettano
>   del tardar mio; ch'io vo' che'l gregge pasca;
>   nè credo che di me pensier si mettano.
> Io ho del pane, e più cose altre in tasca:
>   se vòi star meco, non mi vedrai movere,
>   mentre sarà del vino in questa fiasca:
> e sì potrebbe ben tonare e piovere.*
>
>   (*Opere*, pp. 65–66)

The lovers' complaints left neatly behind, the poet has moved into a moderating landscape with its Virgilian resonance and

---

* MONTANO: Look, it is night, and the whole sky is darkening, and the high mountains shade the countryside; the stars and the moon accompany us. And my sheep are leaving the wood, herded together, since they well know the time and the hour that trouble the flock. Let us follow along, ourselves: since they are going, Uranio, my friend; and already companions are waiting and perhaps fear some harm has overtaken us.

URANIO: Montano, my companions are not fearful for my delay since I wish the flock to feed; nor do I think that anyone is concerned about me. I have bread and many other things in my pockets. If you stay with me, you will not see me leave while there is wine in this flask, even indeed if it thunders and rains.

its lulling terzine (Sannazaro alternates between double and triple rhyme in the passage). The close of the eclogue blends easily into the prose that follows, striking a note most congenial to Sannazaro's poetic talents. Here he pulls out all stops in the creation of atmosphere, describing a moonlight procession with shepherds still under the spell of the songs of Montano and Uranio:

> E così passo passo seguitandole, andavamo per lo silenzio de la serena notte ragionando de le canzoni cantate, e comendando maravigliosamente il novo cominciare di Montano, ma molto più il pronto e securo rispondere di Uranio. . . . Per che ciascuno ringraziava li benigni Dii, che a tanto diletto ne aveano sì impensatamente guidati. E volta avveniva, che mentre noi per via andavamo così parlando, i fiochi fagiani per le loro magioni cantavano.* (*Opere*, pp. 67–68)

The silence is broken only by pheasants and by songs praising the gods for music and poetry.

Sometimes the proses of the Italian *Arcadia* depict rustic festivals and ceremonies in which the poet imagines classical singing contests to have taken place. (There Sannazaro turns to Ovid and the *Fasti* for material.) Several proses simply expand a basic Virgilian situation, the chance meeting of shepherds who join in song. But in all cases the descriptions are organized toward an effect of unbroken harmony and delight. The texture somehow differs from that of Virgil's eclogues. Virgil is still in touch with the realistic bucolic detail of Theocritus. His shepherds contend with some of the harshness of the pastoral world; song for them serves as

---

* And so step by step following them, we went through the silence of the serene night discussing the songs that had been sung, and praising lavishly the original opening of Montano, but much more the quick, confident response of Uranio. . . . For which everyone thanked the generous gods, who had so unexpectedly led us to such delight. And sometimes it happened that while we went along our way talking in this fashion, the hoarse-voiced pheasants sang from their nests.

welcome respite in times that threaten disaster, either man-made (the evictions from the farms in the first eclogue) or natural (the need for shelter from the cold in the seventh). Sannazaro banishes discord from his self-contained world, and his shepherds engage continually in games and song. Goats do not have to be milked; the flocks are mere decorative followers.

The degree to which Sannazaro idealizes the Arcadian landscape is apparent from the book's opening prose description, a set piece of some sixty lines. It contains the elements that were, from the Empire to the sixteenth century, the indispensable features of the *locus amoenus*: trees, a grassy plain, and a fountain or brook.[16] The remarkable thing about the description is not its components, but its astonishing concentration of harmonious detail, its theatricality; Sannazaro loads every rift with ore. He has his delightful plain — with not one tree but twelve or fifteen:

> son forse dodici o quindici alberi di tanto strana et eccessiva bellezza, che chiunque li vedesse, giudicarebbe che la maestra natura vi si fusse con sommo diletto studiata in formarli. Li quali, alquanto distanti et in ordine non artificioso disposti, con la loro rarità la naturale bellezza del luogo oltra misura annobiliscono.*   *(Opere,* p. 51)

The catalogue of exotic and mythical trees that follows this passage is imitated from Ovid *(Met.* x.86). But the listing, already rich in Ovid's version, is embroidered by Sannazaro with epithets borrowed from Virgil,[17] and the simple demonstrative verbs of Ovid *(erat, non abfuit, adfuit)* undergo metamorphoses of their own into graceful amplifications:

---

* There are perhaps twelve or fifteen trees of such strange and exceptional beauty that whoever sees them would judge that masterly nature had been studied with the highest delight in forming them. Being somewhat at a distance and disposed in no artificial order, with their rarity they ennoble the natural beauty of the spot beyond measure.

"oltra misura annobiliscono"; "lo amenissimo platano vi si distendono con le loro ombre." With its ennobling verbs and regular cadences, the passage invites us away from the world of lovers' pains, of distress, rural or urban, into a world evoked by the gentle Italian superlatives: "amenissimo platano"; "drittissimo abete"; "verdissima erbetta"; "con sommo diletto"; "tanto strana et eccessiva bellezza."

The passage does not merely appeal to a feeling for delicate and orderly perfection in nature but, in several different ways, identifies the land of perfect nature as a golden world of poetry. Not only do shepherds' songs resound in all the landscapes of the *Arcadia*; the romance alludes constantly to the metamorphoses of the gods of song in the forests and plains of Arcadia. At the center of Sannazaro's grove rises "un dritto cipresso . . . nel quale non che Ciparisso, ma . . . esso Apollo non si sdegnarebbe essere transfigurato" (a straight cypress into which not only Cyparissus, but Apollo himself would not disdain to be transformed — *Opere*, p. 52). Apollo is present by direct reference; Orpheus, by allusion. The passage from Ovid that Sannazaro imitates in his description of the grove recounts how the music of Orpheus draws a forest of exotic trees to desert places. The metamorphoses Sannazaro alludes to are in themselves only one indication of the staggering density of reference to classical pastoral in the passage. A glance at his editor's notes reveals classical sources for almost every detail and trick of expression. Sannazaro's concentrated references must have had the force of highly charged superlatives for sixteenth-century readers. The effect is to add another dimension to an already intense atmosphere and to blend with the appeal of ideal landscape the sentiment attached to memories of classical pastoral scenes.

In such hypnotic settings, lovers lamenting in the Petrarchan manner can scarcely style themselves "solo e pensoso."

Sannazaro's third eclogue, which resembles in many ways Petrarch's love poems, is performed at a rustic festival where the main recreation is the singing of "amorose canzoni." Bands of nymphs weave garlands of delicate flowers. Galicio, the singer of the eclogue, begins the lyric so sweetly that all are silenced, and, when he finishes, the mood is prolonged in praises of his voice ("piena di armonia inestimabile") and of his style ("suavissimo e dolce"). The eclogue itself should be examined with care, for its technique is representative of the love poetry of the *Arcadia*. Sannazaro casts it in the form of a canzone of six stanzas, deriving its meter and rhyme scheme quite carefully from Petrarch.[18] The critical question is, how well does he echo the Petrarchan voice?

In a very simple lyric, the shepherd singer, after a stanza placing him in the usual wood beside a stream, praises the day, the third day of March, which is the birthday of his mistress Amaranta. He begs Apollo to bring May days before their season and invokes a vision of the Golden Age to return in Amaranta's honor:

> Valli vicine, e rupi,
> cipressi, alni, et abeti,
> porgete orecchie a le mie basse rime;
> e non teman de' lupi
> gli agnelli mansueti;
> ma torni il mondo a quelle usanze prime.
> Fioriscan per le cime
> i cerri in bianche rose;
> e per le spine dure
> pendan l'uve mature:
> suden di mel le querce alte e nodose;
> e le fontane intatte
> corran di puro latte.
> Nascan erbette e fiori,
> e li fieri animali
> lassen le loro asprezze e i petti crudi:

> vegnan li vaghi amori
> senza fiammelle o strali
> scherzando inseme, pargoletti e 'gnudi:
> poi con tutti lor studi
> canten le bianche Nimfe,
> e con abiti strani
> salten Fauni e Silvani:
> ridan li prati, e le correnti limfe;
> e non si vedan oggi
> nuvoli intorno ai poggi.*

(Opere, pp. 74–75)

This kind of vision, familiar to readers of Petrarch as a pastoral metaphor for the poet's new life, is given point in the following stanza, which praises Amaranta's purity. Like Astraea she is the last refuge of virtue in a blind world. An account of the lover's predicament follows; he carves her name on the trunks of trees and complains at the close of the poem in the expected contraries of the wars of love:

> sempre fia noto il nome,
> le man, gli occhi e le chiome
> di quella che mi fa sì lunga guerra;
> per cui quest'aspra amara
> vita m'è dolce e cara.†

(Opere, p. 76)

The energy of the poem lies in the central two stanzas;

* Nearby valleys and cliffs, cypresses, alders, and firs, listen to my humble verses; and gentle lambs shall not fear the wolves; but the world shall return to its first ways. Oaks shall blossom in white roses on the mountain tops; and ripe grapes hang from harsh thorns; high knotty oaks shall sweat honey, and untouched springs run with pure milk. Grasses and flowers shall spring up, and wild animals lose their harshness and cruel hearts. Pretty Loves shall come without flames or arrows, playing together, naked babes. Then with all their graces the white nymphs shall sing, and with their strange habits fauns and wood-creatures shall leap. Meadows shall laugh, along with the running sap, and no clouds shall be seen around the hills today.

† Forever shall be known the name, the hands, the eyes, and the hair of the one who gives me so long a war; for whom this harsh bitter life is to me sweet and dear.

their pastoral vision richly figures the perfection that Galicio sees in his mistress. But the tone of delight that dominates the poem does not blend easily with a passage that immediately follows the singer's praise of Amaranta: "quella per cui sospiro, / per cui piango e m'adiro," the one for whom I sigh, for whom I weep and grow angry. Despite the Petrarchan vocabulary and phrasing,[19] the dramatic situation in which such phrases validly express the lover's state has not been prepared with Petrarch's delicacy. Enacted in this setting the Petrarchan laments appear irrelevant. What Sannazaro lacks in this eclogue is the imaginative conception that, in Petrarch's lyric meditations, links exhaustion and melancholy to his joyful visions of love. The slender eclogue from the *Arcadia* yields instead to a rhetorical temptation that manages to make it an attractive poem; Sannazaro in the central stanzas echoes several earlier versions of the Golden Age. The most familiar references are to Virgil [20] and to Ovid, but he also draws upon Horace and Tibullus. The sheer pleasure in harmony and in outdoing any single classical pastoral by echoing many — and this pleasure is a strength of the *Arcadia* — is also enough to overshadow, to absorb and render pointless, the conventional lover's lament.

In the fourth eclogue of the *Arcadia*, a fine double sestina that, as we shall see, Sidney must have known well, Sannazaro attends in a more complex manner to the balance of complaint and redeeming pastoral vision. Logisto's opening invitation, "Chi vuole udire i miei sospiri in rime," forecasts accurately the content of the poem to follow; the phrase "sospiri in rime," sighs in verse, does not serve here simply as a formulaic repetition of a characteristic phrase from Petrarch.[21] The lament, sung in alternate strophes by Logisto and Elpino, is based upon the Petrarchan motif of the enclosed valley, with its traditional view of pastoral retreat as symbolic of the lover's meditations upon his state. They emphasize in the first half of the poem only the melancholy aspects of the lover's self-exile: his hopeless wandering and the prison that love has made of his thoughts. The double sestina provides exactly the right form for this extended lament, and we may sense its strength from the first few stanzas:

LOG: Chi vuole udire i miei sospiri in rime,
   donne mie care, e l'angoscioso pianto,
   e quanti passi tra la notte e 'l giorno
   spargendo indarno vo per tanti campi;
   legga per queste querce e per li sassi,
   che n'è già piena omai ciascuna valle.

ELP: Pastori, ucel nè fiera alberga in valle,
   che non conosca il suon de le mie rime;
   nè spelunca o caverna è fra gli sassi,
   che non rimbombe al mio continuo pianto;
   nè fior nè erbetta nasce in questi campi,
   ch'io no la calche mille volte il giorno.

LOG: Lasso, ch'io non so ben l'ora nè 'l giorno,
   che fui rinchiuso in questa alpestra valle;
   nè mi ricordo mai correr per campi
   libero o sciolto; ma piangendo in rime
   sempre in fiamme son visso; e col mio pianto
   ho pur mosso a pietà gli alberi e i sassi.*

             (*Opere*, p. 83)

* LOG: Whoever wishes to hear my sighs in verse, my dear ladies, and the anguished lament, and how many steps both night and day I pace out in vain as I go through so many fields; let him read them in these oaks and rocks, since every valley is already so full of them.

ELP: No shepherd, bird, or beast dwells in the valley who does not know the sound of my verses; nor is there a cave or hollow among the rocks that does not resound with my unbroken lament; nor is there a flower or grass that springs up in these fields that I do not tread upon a thousand times a day.

LOG: Alas, that I do not even know the hour or the day when I was shut into this mountainous valley; nor do I remember ever running through the fields free and untrammeled; but, weeping in verse, I have always lived in flames; and with my lament I have even moved the trees and the rocks to pity.

Although Sannazaro draws many phrases of the complaint directly from Petrarch, his poetic success lies in his using the double sestina so well. Sestine do occur relatively often in Italian poetry, but the double sestina is rarely attempted. Petrarch essays the form only once in the *Rime*, in a lament for the death of Laura, and there treats it as somewhat of a curiosity ("e doppiando 'l dolor, doppia lo stile"),[22] allowing the double length to symbolize a doubled sorrow. Sannazaro finds the strength of the form in its repetitions. In particular he chooses his verse endings carefully: two, *rime* and *pianto*, to characterize the lover's activity in song; three, *campi, sassi*, and *valle*, to characterize the repeated bleakness of experience in the recurring landmarks of the enclosed valley. The repetition of these words, combined with the sixth, *giorno*, used also to measure the inescapable round of daily wanderings, reinforces the lovers' experience in the opening half of the poem — their inability to remember the day when they had been put into this landscape or the time when they ran free in the meadows.

In the exact center of the poem, the point at which the first cycle of rhymes is completed and the poetic material appears to be exhausted, Elpino's tone changes suddenly from despair to joy. No dramatic reason is given; a voice from among the rocks promises hope and good fortune, presumably in love, "un lieto fausto aventuroso giorno." The pairings of stanzas in the second half of the contest then oppose the voices of the two shepherds to one another — Logisto asserting his despair more strongly, Elpino his growing joy. The shift does not emerge logically from the content of the poem, but it does permit Sannazaro to exercise through Elpino the harmonious pastoral mode that tempts him so often in the romance. Logisto prefers to be a specter at Elpino's pastoral feast:

ELP: Deh, se ciò fusse, or qual mai piaggia o valle
        udrebbe tante o sì suavi rime?
        Certo io farei saltare i boschi e i sassi,
        sì com'un tempo Orfeo col dolce pianto:
        allor si sentirebbon per li campi
        torturelle e colombe in ogni giorno.

LOG: Allora io cheggio che sovente il giorno
        il mio sepolcro onori in questa valle:
        e le ghirlande colte a' verdi campi,
        al cener muto dii con le tue rime,
        dicendo: — Alma infelice, che di pianto
        vivesti un tempo, or posa in questi sassi —.

ELP: Logisto, odanlo i fiumi, odanlo i sassi,
        che un lieto fausto aventuroso giorno
        s'apparecchia a voltarti in riso il pianto;
        se pur l'erbe ch'io colsi a la mia valle
        non m'ingannaro, e le 'ncantate rime,
        che di biade più volte han privi i campi.*

                                    (*Opere*, pp. 84–85)

The two voices of the poem are never reconciled; nor does the note of hope swallow up the lover's complaint in the way that the vision of the Golden Age obscures it in the third eclogue. This double sestina represents Sannazaro at his best in love poetry. He pays more than lip service to the lament of the Petrarchan lover: both in this form with its repetitions and

* ELP: Ah, if that may be, now what shore or valley will have heard so many or such gentle verses? Certainly I would make the woods and rocks leap, as once Orpheus did with his sweet lament. Then in the fields turtle-doves and pigeons would be heard every day.

LOG: Now I ask that oftentimes you honor my grave in this valley, and that you offer garlands gathered from the green fields along with your verses beside my silent ashes, saying, "Unfortunate soul, who once lived, lamenting, now lie among these rocks."

ELP: Logisto, let the streams hear and the rocks hear that a joyful, blessed, fortunate day is being prepared, to turn your lament to laughter, if indeed the grass that I have gathered in my valley, and my verses of incantation, which have robbed the fields of grain many times, do not deceive me.

in the accents of individual lines, he captures the qualities of
exhaustion and destructive desire, which are one aspect of the
experience Petrarch described. These tones identify the
voice of Logisto and of Elpino in the first half of the poem
before his "conversion."

That kind of complaint can be conveyed well in the dominant verse form of the *Arcadia*'s eclogues, the *terzina sdrucciola*
(or *terza rima* using triple rhymes). When Sannazaro chooses
to invoke the mood of fierce melancholy, he can do so with the
"dying fall" of the triple rhyme, which is even more effective
than that of the feminine rhyme he uses in the double
sestina:

> Primavera e suoi dì per me non riedono,
> nè truovo erbe o fioretti che mi gioveno;
> ma solo pruni e stecchi che 'l cor ledono.
> Nubbi mai da quest'aria non si moveno,
> e veggio, quando i dì son chiari e tepidi,
> notti di verno, che tonando pioveno.
> Perisca il mondo, e non pensar ch'io trepidi;
> ma attendo sua ruina, e già considero
> che'l cor s'adempia di pensier più lepidi.*
>
> (Opere, pp. 54–55)

But the dominant voice of the *Arcadia* is not the voice of
the man for whom spring will not return and for whom the
ruins of a world hold no terrors. Although Sannazaro weighs
the lover's pains against the joy of pastoral imagination, as
Petrarch does, he resolves contradictions most often with an
accent like Elpino's in the concluding section of the double
sestina:

* For me spring and its days do not return, nor do I find grass and
flowers that I would enjoy, but only thorn bushes and thorns that injure the
heart. Clouds never move from this sky, and I see, when the days are clear
and warm, winter nights that thunder and rain. Let the world perish, and
do not think that I would tremble, for I expect its ruin, and anticipate already that my heart will be filled with more sprightly thoughts.

Certo io farei saltare i boschi e i sassi,
sì com'un tempo Orfeo col dolce pianto:
allor si sentirebbon per li campi
torturelle e colombe in ogni giorno.

His joy comes from realization of his own powers; like Orpheus, he draws woods and stones to dance to his music. Unhappy lovers become great poets.

Again and again Sannazaro returns to the figure of Orpheus and to the theme of metamorphosis.[23] The tenth prose recounts a myth of the descent of pastoral poetry. Pan's amorous pursuit of Syrinx spurs her transformation into a shepherd's pipe. The Ovidian tale is recalled with the relish that Marvell was to take in it: "And *Pan* did after *Syrinx* speed, / Not as a Nymph, but for a Reed." In Sannazaro's more explicit gloss, "i sospiri si convertirono in dolce suono," sighs transformed themselves into sweet sound. Pan's lyric strength passes to Theocritus, who has the Orphic powers, who moves pines and oaks with his music, and who finds in nature the mirror of his own harmonious song. His skill descends in turn to Virgil and finally, one assumes, to the shepherds of the Italian *Arcadia*. The myth springs from the experience of all lovers who wander into Arcadia. When Sincero finishes a long prose lament recounting in great detail his sorrows in love, the shepherd Carino responds with a few words of compassion and many in praise of his fine singing. He rewards him with a special *sampogna* in the hope that Sincero will, in a higher style, be among the great poets of his century and win eternal fame. A gesture like Carino's lures the reader away from the content of the song toward admiration for the gesture of singing and the perfections of form. The special power of Sannazaro's *Arcadia* rests in its being a paradise for poets. His ideal landscape dissolves the lover's pains with an ease and a self-admiration that may disturb the reader's sense of appropriateness at the same time that its rhetoric teases him out of thought.

3

The reasons for the popularity of Sannazaro's *Arcadia* in the sixteenth century are clear. Its richness as a poetic source-book is in part a function of its eclecticism. Sannazaro refers with such frequency to the classics of pastoral literature that his *Arcadia* calls up a wide range of dramatic attitudes associated with that genre. His eclogues, it is true, seldom touch the dramatic occasion that seems to have inspired them — whether it is love, death, or political distress. In his love poetry (eight of the eclogues qualify as love poems) the contributing voices, particularly the Virgilian shepherd and the Petrarchan poet-lover, are only loosely combined in verse that does not bear the impress of a strong shaping poetic personality. But it is possible that, if Sannazaro's own skill at dramatizing had been a firmer one, his work would not have attracted poets with as widely differing sensibilities as Ronsard and Sidney. As it is, the Italian *Arcadia* offers material for a variety of attitudes toward the complaining lover. Sannazaro's work is available to poets who adopt his mise-en-scène as an immediately recognizable stage for the particular comedy or drama of love they wish to see enacted. His eclogues provide a primer of topics, of rhetorical poses for the lover. The degree to which desire plays a part, the degree to which absorption into the ideal landscape is allowed to modify the lover's pain — these vary with the outlook of the imitating poet.

The Renaissance poet could also accept Sannazaro's re-creation of the Virgilian Arcadia as a landscape in which poetic invention is a recognized and honored activity. Sannazaro sets a precedent of concern with intricacy of form: canzoni, sestine, ingenious metrical combinations, and above all the perfection of the *terzina sdrucciola*. His model provides ample encouragement for a poet like Sidney who uses the Arcadian setting as background for poetic experiments in Italian and classical forms. If we need any further assurance that Sidney knew the Italian work, it lies in his often disastrous adoption of the *terzina sdrucciola* as a standard eclogue form, and in his fruitful study of Sannazaro's double sestina.

For Sannazaro in his *Arcadia* the pastoral world suffices in itself: "certo egli è migliore il poco terreno ben coltivare, che'l molto lasciare per mal governo miseramente imboschire," better to cultivate a small parcel of land well than to let a large one, through neglect, grow wild and woody (*Opere*, p. 50). But, in the Renaissance, pastoral was constantly moving into conjunction with other genres in ever-changing combinations. We need only remember Polonius' kaleidoscopic catalogue of genres to guess at the possibilities. Once the symbolic value of Arcadia was established, poets began to measure it against other worlds, particularly against the heroic. Sidney does precisely that in his *Arcadia*.

HEROIC AND PASTORAL

S IDNEY'S VAST *Arcadia*, prose and poetry, heroic and pastoral, draws on a variety of sources and materials, but its poetry is almost exclusively love poetry, sung or recited in settings that derive their elaborate harmony from Sannazaro. Milton's extreme description — he called the English *Arcadia* "vain" and "amatorious" — is in some ways relevant.[1] His severity, of course, grows out of his own polemical purpose in *Eikonoklastes*: a prayer drawn from such a tale as Sidney's ("a heathen fiction praying to a heathen god") was hardly suitable for Charles I on the scaffold. For Milton the *Arcadia* was "a book in that kind full of worth and wit, but among religious thoughts and duties not worthy to be named; nor to be read at any time without good caution." The Puritan's uneasiness about Arcadian love in literature suggests some of the difficulties that Sidney, active Protestant statesman that he was, also might have felt in adapting elements of the cloistered world of Italian pastoral to his English romance. The charge of "lightness and wantonness" was one that sixteenth-century English critics had to meet. According to Sir John Harington, one of these apologists, in the preface to his translation of Ariosto, "lightness and wantonness" was an "objection of some importance, sith as Sir Philip Sidney confesseth, *Cupido* is crept even into the heroicall Poemes, and consequently makes that also subject to this reproofe." [2]

It is a curious fact about the English *Arcadia* that Sidney, while obviously concerned with love, displays a marked distrust of *otium*, of pastoral repose, of the conventional ways of dramatizing the pursuits of love. Sidney continually refers us to a framework of heroic adventure. He begins his romance, both in its original version and in the revised version first published in 1590,[3] at the point where the heroes, Pyrocles and Musidorus, reaching Arcadia, abandon their heroic responsibilities for the love of the Arcadian princesses, Philoclea and Pamela. Nevertheless, in both versions of the work, the epic narrative — in flashbacks — is interwoven with the progress of the pastoral romance. When Homer was not at hand, according to Gabriel Harvey, one might "read his furious Iliads and cunning Odysses in the brave adventures of Pyrocles and Musidorus." [4] Fulke Greville made even graver claims for Sidney's heroic examples. In them he saw, beyond ferocious and cunning action, the force of moral instruction:

> his purpose was to limn out such exact pictures, of every posture in the minde, that any man being forced, in the straines of this life, to pass through any straights, or latitudes of good, or ill fortune, might (as in a glasse) see how to set a good countenance upon all the discountenances of adversitie, and a stay upon the exorbitant smilings of chance.[5]

The extravagance of heroic demands distinguishes Pyrocles and Musidorus from Sincero in Sannazaro's *Arcadia*. They may change their names and take on disguises when they enter Sidney's pastoral world, but they cannot change their natures. We are aware of their responsibilities to the world of action not only when they tell stories of their adventurous pasts, but also when they lament forsaking the active life, having been brought low by love in *Arcadia*: "Then power

[pour] out plaint, and in one word say this: / Helples his plaint, who spoyles himselfe of blisse." [6]

The explicit invitation to measure pastoral love against heroic achievement is a characteristic source of energy and delight, of fierce argument and comic predicament, in the *Arcadia*. The problem itself is hardly new, but Sidney's treatment has a different flavor from, to take an obvious example, the easy movement from heroic feat to pastoral temptation in *Orlando Furioso*. Sidney punctuates such contrasts with deliberate debates; characters in the *Arcadia* analyze their situations with all the passionate command of characters in Racine. While they are fully responsive to love, their responsibilities to a hero's training remain pressing: constant vigilance and constant pursuit of noble achievement. They think it "not so worthy, to be brought to heroycall effects by fortune, or necessitie (like *Ulysses* and *Aeneas*) as by ones owne choice, and working" (*F*, I.206). It is no wonder, then, that Sidney's version of pastoral love is a peculiar one and that the complaints of lovers in his *Arcadia* are not absorbed or mellowed by the harmonious landscape as they are in Sannazaro's. The discussion of the poetry of Sidney's *Arcadia* in the next chapter should be more meaningful after we have looked at that poetry — not only its content but its form — as part of Sidney's enduring dramatic concern, the relation of love to the demands of the active life.

1

The *Arcadia* is not Sidney's first venture in writing pastoral; what he was to do on a large scale in the romance is anticipated in important ways by an earlier work, his pastoral masque performed before Queen Elizabeth on her visit to the Earl of Leicester at Wanstead in May 1578.[7] This slight but illuminating work, which we know as *The Lady of May*, was printed for the first time at the end of the folio of 1598. We have, not an author's scenario, but a description of the masque as presented:

HER MOST EXCELLENT MAJESTIE WALKING IN WANSTEED GARDEN, AS SHE PASSED DOWNE INTO THE grove, there came suddenly among the traine, one apparelled like an honest mans wife of the countrey, where crying out for justice . . . she was brought to the presence of her Majestie, to whom upon her knees she offred a supplication. (*F*, II.329)

"A brace, a couple, a cast of young men," are claiming the hand of the Lady of May, the daughter of the honest country wife who asks for the queen's aid in settling the strife between the two suitors. Readers of this masque will know the figure of the schoolmaster Rombus who appears early, seizing delightedly on the quarrel as an opportunity for rhetorical display before the queen. Like Holofernes in *Love's Labour's Lost*, for whom he is said to have been a model, he "draweth out the thread of his verbosity finer than the staple of his argument." But the resemblance between the two figures suggests a more interesting relationship between the masque and Shakespeare's play. Both works share a playful attitude not only toward the abuses of rhetoric, but also toward the extravagances of pastoral. The witty impulse behind *The Lady of May* becomes clearer when the lady herself, impatient with the "good Latine foole," interrupts Rombus and introduces to the queen the choice she is being asked to make.[8] The May Lady shears Rombus' flowers of rhetoric with a delicately balanced rhetoric of her own, which, by comparison with his, sounds fresh and direct. She presents her suitors, conventional pastoral figures — Therion, a forester, and Espilus, a shepherd — in quite a special way:

I like them both, and love neither, *Espilus* is the richer, but *Therion* the livelier; *Therion* doth me many pleasures, as stealing me venison out of these forrests, and many other such like prettie and prettier services, but withall he growes to such rages, that sometimes he strikes me, sometimes he railes at me. This shepheard *Espilus* of a mild disposition, as his fortune hath not bene to do me great service, so hath he never done me any wrong, but feeding his sheepe, sitting under some sweete bush, sometimes they say he records my name in dolefull verses. Now the question I am to aske you faire Ladie, is, whether the many deserts and many faults of *Therion,* or the verie small deserts and no faults of *Espilus* be to be preferred. (*F*, II.332–333)

The masque is moving toward the traditional pastoral singing contest with the May Lady herself as prize, but her description of the contestants sets the reader slightly off balance; for Espilus, with little but his riches to recommend him, seems a sad and somewhat comic shepherd rather than a "true pastoralist." [9] Neither he nor Therion (who fulfills the promise of wildness in his name) is the ideal suitor, but Therion's vigor serves as a direct criticism of the passive shepherd. The shrewd psychological insight into each suitor, particularly the glimpse of the violence that is the counterpart of Therion's liveliness, lends dramatic point and suspense to the singing contest that follows. There, parallel stanzas enforce Sidney's contrast. Espilus boasts:

> Two thousand sheepe I have as white as milke,
> Though not so white as is thy lovely face,
> The pasture rich, the wooll as soft as silke,
> All this I give, let me possesse thy grace,
> But still take heede least thou thy selfe submit
> To one that hath no wealth, and wants his wit.

Therion's reply makes the shepherd look slightly ridiculous. The forester makes capital of his own poverty as he redefines wealth and its relation to love:

> Two thousand deere in wildest woods I have,
> Them can I take, but you I cannot hold:
> He is not poore who can his freedome save,

Bound but to you, no wealth but you I would:
But take this beast, if beasts you feare to misse,
For of his beasts the greatest beast he is.

(*LM*, 2.19–30)

Espilus has complimented her beauty; Therion, her vitality and the power she holds over him. There is certainly an ironic view taken of the possessive Espilus. But, for the moment, neither of the suitors gains a decisive victory, and the masque proceeds to its real point, a general argument about the respective merits of the active and the contemplative life. As the May Lady says to the queen, "in judging me, you judge more than me in it."

Dorcas, an old shepherd, defends the life of the herdsman with traditional and attractive arguments. The shepherd, unlike the courtier, he argues, leads a life free of ambition, "neither subject to violent oppression, nor servile flatterie." Among the flocks "it is lawfull for a man to be good if he list . . . where the eye may be busied in considering the works of nature, and the hart quietly rejoyced in the honest using them" (*F*, II.335). So far the argument would be more than familiar to an Elizabethan audience.

The shepherd's opponent, Rixus, a young forester, agrees that goodness can be found in the life that Dorcas describes. But, Rixus continues, the forester's life includes not only "countrey quietnesse," but also "gallant . . . activity" that "doth both strengthen the body, and raise up the mind." Here one recognizes one of Sidney's recurring themes: there is no real split between the active and the contemplative lives; activity too is necessary to "raise up the mind." The prose rises to a marked climax as Rixus shows how the life of the forester embodies a particular nobility of ambition:

O sweet contentation to see the long life of the hurtlesse trees, to see how in streight growing up, though never so high, they hinder not their fellowes, they only enviously trouble, which are crookedly bent. What life is to be compared to ours where the very growing things are ensamples of goodnesse?

(F, II.336–337)

The life he envisions is inclusive: thought grows smoothly into action. Rixus turns then to love, commenting ironically on the conventional melancholy shepherd and his "doleful verses":

we have no hopes, but we may quickly go about them, and going about them, we soone obtaine them; not like those that have long followed one (in troth) most excellent chace, do now at length perceive she could never be taken: but that if she stayed at any time neare the pursuers, it was never meant to tarry with them, but only to take breath to fly further from them. (F, II.337)

Having heard the arguments, the queen is asked to make her decision: there is some suggestion that Sidney expected her to choose the forester, "well deserving and painefull Therion," over "idle Espilus" since the masque closes with a song celebrating the victory of Silvanus, the forest god. The shepherd's party is consoled with a brief tale in the Ovidian manner to demonstrate that Pan can be proud to have been defeated in love by so worthy a foe as Hercules (who is meant here to represent activity).

One of the difficulties in reading the masque is that, although everything does point to a victory for the forester, Queen Elizabeth actually chose the shepherd Espilus. Since the account declines to print the queen's words, one finds her decision hard to understand.[10] Perhaps Sidney's unorthodox treatment of pastoral convention went unnoticed, and the queen chose the shepherd as the usual representative of the contemplative life; royalty has been known to nod before and since.

What is important for the reader of the *Arcadia*, at any rate, is the way in which Sidney attempts to reinterpret traditional notions of pastoral retirement. The audience is asked to think again about the qualities needed for the life of contemplation and the literary symbols used to represent it. Sidney accomplishes this not by completely rejecting the symbolic shepherd, but by projecting his life attractively and seeing some value in its implied criticism of the court. He then suggests that knowledge of pastoral quiet must somehow join itself to the virtuous activity of the forester. Whatever contradictions exist between the two lives are resolved for the moment in the emblem of the growing "hurtlesse trees."

Sidney's distrust of *otium* makes itself felt in a work as simple as *The Lady of May*; in Rixus the forester he makes a gesture toward the heroic figures of Pyrocles and Musidorus in the *Arcadia*. Of course, the ideal that Rixus represents is only suggested in the masque, its complexities not really explored. The rewards of love in the forest at Wanstead follow naturally for the man who leads the good life. But in the *Arcadia* the world of love is presented as more complicated, with benefits and demands of its own. Coming to Arcadia is a mixed blessing to the princes from Thessaly and Macedon.

2

In the first book of the *Arcadia* Sidney concerns himself with the dramatic complications of heroes falling in love. On a grander scale than in *The Lady of May*, he tests conventional assumptions about pastoral leisure. But here the issue is not so much the relative values of the active and the contemplative life as it is the values of heroic quest set against amatory adventure in Arcadia. To put it so barely, of course, does no justice to Sidney's wit and the subtleties of his method. For though these opposing attitudes toward the entrance of the heroes into Arcadia provide material for serious debate, they often emerge in playful fashion or in dramatic situations that qualify rigid rhetorical positions.

There is one particularly adroit use of a pastoral convention that may illustrate the point. Shortly after his rescue by Kalander from the shipwreck that opens the *Arcadia*, Pyrocles sees a portrait of the princess Philoclea and falls instantly in love with her. He takes to solitary wanderings that alarm the vigilant, and still unwounded, Musidorus. Finally Pyrocles disappears, and Musidorus begins a long search for him. At one point, fatigued and on the edge of sleep, Musidorus is surprised by the sight of an Amazon lady. The episode in outline has a familiar ring: an attractive lady suddenly appears to the questing hero in a moment of repose; she vanishes, not seeing him, into a "fine close arbour: it was of trees whose branches so lovingly interlaced one the other, that it could resist the strongest violence of eye-sight." Sidney describes the Amazon lavishly and makes her a seductive example of the collaboration of art and nature:

> Well might he perceave the hanging of her haire in fairest quantitie, in locks, some curled, and some as it were forgotten, with such a carelesse care, and an arte so hiding arte, that she seemed she would lay them for a paterne, whether nature simply, or nature helped by cunning, be more excellent: the rest whereof was drawne into a coronet of golde richly set with pearle, and so joyned all over with gold wiers, and covered with feathers of divers colours, that it was not unlike to an helmet, such a glittering shew it bare, and so bravely it was held up from the head. (*F*, I.75)

The description continues, taking the reader through intricate details, comparisons, and qualifications. Musidorus is caught up, follows her to her arbor "as warely as he could," and overhears her singing "with a voice no lesse beautifull

[48]

to his eares, than her goodlinesse was full of harmonie to his eyes."

But the song he overhears undermines the entire vision: he recognizes that the singing Amazon is Pyrocles in disguise. With the swiftest of reversals we find ourselves back in the world of stern heroic values. To Musidorus, his friend's transformation into the handsome forest lady becomes an emblem of weakness:

> And is it possible, that this is *Pyrocles*, the onely yong Prince in the world, formed by nature, and framed by education, to the true exercise of vertue? . . . Remember (for I know you know it) that if we wil be men, the reasonable parte of our soule, is to have absolute commaundement; against which if any sensuall weaknes arise, we are to yeelde all our sounde forces to the overthrowing of so unnaturall a rebellion, wherein how can we wante courage, since we are to deale against so weake an adversary, that in it selfe is nothinge but weakenesse? (*F*, I.77)

Of course, the humor of the scene lies in the fact that Musidorus, who has turned preacher and is prepared to denounce love, had himself been attracted to the Amazon. Sidney underlines the effect by presenting everything from Musidorus' point of view, allowing the reader to be attracted, deceived, and surprised in much the same way that Musidorus is. "Amazedly looking upon him (as *Apollo* is painted when he saw *Daphne* sodainly turned into a Laurell) he was not able to bring forth a worde." The mythological reference does double service: it lends resonance to Musidorus' surprise and grief, but also it reminds us of his complicated situation. Like Apollo, he sees his pastoral dalliance turning into something else, in this case sorrow for his friend's transformation and a feeling that he must rebuke him.

This episode typifies the tension that Sidney so deftly

maintains between the demands of the heroic life and the inroads of passion. He participates in the elaborate delights of Arcadia and realizes their danger. The same kind of amusing counterpoint lies behind the debates that form a large part of the first book, as the heroes self-consciously weigh opinions about falling in love. Even before he runs away to assume his disguise as an Amazon, Pyrocles must respond to Musidorus' charges that he has given over worthy enterprises: "you let your minde fal a sleepe . . . and . . . you subject your selfe to solitarines, the slye enimie, that doth most separate a man from well doing." Pyrocles adroitly replies:

> I must needes say thus much, my deere cosin, that I find not my selfe wholye to be condemned, because I do not with continuall vehemency folow those knowledges, which you call the bettering of my minde; for both the minde it selfe must (like other thinges) sometimes be unbent, or else it will be either weakned, or broken: And these knowledges, as they are of good use, so are they not all the minde may stretch it selfe unto: who knowes whether I feede not my minde with higher thoughts? . . . And in such contempla-tion . . . I enjoye my solitarines . . . Eagles we see fly alone; and they are but sheepe, which alwaies heard together; con-demne not therefore my minde somtime to enjoy it selfe; nor blame not the taking of such times as serve most fitte for it. (*F*, I.56)

He becomes eloquent about the Arcadian landscape: "Is not every *eccho* thereof a perfect Musicke? and these fresh and delightful brookes how slowly they slide away, as loth to leave the company of so many things united in perfection?" Finally he comes to the point that might reveal to Musidorus the reason for his hyperbolic vision of their new lives:

> Certainelie, certainely, cosin, it must needes be that some God-desse enhabiteth this Region, who is the soule of this soile:

for neither is any, lesse then a Goddesse, worthie to be shrined in such a heap of pleasures: nor any lesse then a Goddesse, could have made it so perfect a plotte of the celestiall dwellings.   (*F*, I.57)

The appearance of Pyrocles belies his eloquence and the harmonious vision of contemplation he is trying to present. Musidorus can "see in his countenance some great determination mixed with feare; and might perceive in him store of thoughts, rather stirred then digested." With wry common sense, Musidorus points out that, although he admires Pyrocles' words, he finds his praise of Arcadia excessive: Thessaly and Macedon are equally beautiful, and Pyrocles' eloquence resembles too closely the words that poets give to "these fantasticall mind-infected people, that children and Musitians cal Lovers."

As this counterpointing of values continues through Book One, it provides a full and delightful framework of opinion about love, a moral preparation for what is to follow in the romance. Musidorus, with his sober rebukes, steadily loses ground; if he experiences a moment of weakness at the sight of the Amazon, seeing Pamela completely undoes him. He learns for himself the strength of the adversaries of the "reasonable parte of our soule." But the viewpoint that he had begun by representing is one to which Sidney gives great weight in the heroic sections of the *Arcadia*. The life of honor — harmonious with the life of reason — requires perpetual alertness and must be continually renewed or else it falls away. Love, at least at the outset, is likened explicitly to the misfortunes the princes meet in their heroic lives, misfortunes like the shipwreck and piracy that open the romance. Musidorus laments Pyrocles' lovelorn state: "Heretofore I have accused the sea, condemned the Pyrats, and hated my evill fortune, that deprived me of thee; But now thy self is the sea, which drounes my comfort, thy selfe is the Pirat that robbes thy selfe of me: Thy owne will becomes my evill fortune" (*F*, I.61). If love will prove later to be a beacon to virtue, neither the haven of marriage nor that of Platonic love is here in sight. Pastoral adventure first leads the princes into comic mishap and oratorical declamation.

Arcadia for Pyrocles and Musidorus is not, then, a land of innocent enjoyment, but one of complex experience. The princes complain not only of frustrated love, as Sannazaro's shepherds do, but of lost honor. Much of the poetry of Sidney's *Arcadia* reflects the plight of speakers of high conscience who have entered a world in which there is leisure for love. While nothing in the verses quoted below is as complicated as the witty turnabouts of Sidney's prose in the Amazon scene, the pressure of judgment touches even the slightest lyrics. Here Musidorus, now in love with the princess Pamela, refers to his disguise as a shepherd, his way of entering the court and observing her:

> Come shepheard's weedes, become your master's minde:
> Yeld outward shew, what inward change he tryes:
> Nor be abasht, since such a guest you finde,
> Whose strongest hope in your weake comfort lyes.
>
> Come shepheard's weedes, attend my woefull cryes:
> Disuse your selves from sweete *Menalcas'* voice:
> For other be those tunes which sorrow tyes,
> From those cleere notes which freely may rejoyce.
> Then power out plaint, and in one word say this:
> Helples his plaint, who spoyles himselfe of blisse.
>
> (*Arc.* 4)

In a manner appropriate to Musidorus, the song balances a sense of loss of the world of action ("inward change") with a wry acceptance of "shepheard's weedes." Almost abstractly it identifies the role of shepherd and·plaintive lover with "weake comfort" and a sadly transformed mind. The speaker assumes the role of shepherd, but his tones are not those of sweet Menalcas; the careful oppositions out of which the complaint is constructed remind us that he has loyalties and responsibilities elsewhere that conflict with these first feelings of love. Here, in other words, we find no innocent surprise at the pains of love and wild games of Cupid. Musidorus lays the responsibility upon himself, the knight "who spoyles himselfe of blisse." Nor is there a striking off of a single attitude of suffering as in Shakespeare's song:

> Come away, come away, death,
> And in sad cypress let me be laid.
> Fly away, fly away, breath,
> I am slain by a fair cruel maid:
>> My shroud of white, stuck all with yew, O prepare it,
>> My part of death, no one so true did share it.

Musidorus' song, by contrast, sounds like an intellectual prologue to a pastoral lament. He speaks with considered gravity, referring us to personal honor in a manner we have come to understand through French classical tragedy.

3

Before turning to a detailed consideration of Sidney's Arcadian poems, we might see more of their special quality by considering as a contrast the pastoral adventures of Sir Calidore, the Knight of Courtesy, in Book Six of *The Faerie Queene*. Calidore's "doffing his bright armes" and dressing in shepherd's weeds to woo his lady, Pastorella, is portrayed as a much more innocent act than the disguisings of Pyrocles and Musidorus. For Spenser repose does not, at least in Book Six, signify a slackening of the will, and love complements the

[53]

heroic life without endangering it. Hence Spenser can say of
Calidore:

> Another quest, another game in vew
> He hath, the guerdon of his love to gaine:
> With whom he myndes for ever to remaine,
> And set his rest amongst the rusticke sort,
>
> . . . . .
>
> Ne certes mote he greatly blamed be,
>   From so high step to stoupe unto so low.
>   For who had tasted once (as oft did he)
>   The happy peace, which there doth overflow,
>   And prov'd the perfect pleasures, which doe grow
>   Amongst poore hyndes, in hils, in woods, in dales,
>   Would never more delight in painted show
>   Of such false blisse, as there is set for stales,
> T'entrap unwary fooles in their eternall bales.[11]

To justify pastoral love, the heroic quest is for the moment
deplored as a "hunt still after shadowes vaine / of courtly
favour."

The poetic center of the pastoral episode is, of course, the
vision of the Graces dancing in Venus' favorite haunt, Mount
Acidale, to the piping of Colin Clout. Calidore discovers "an
hundred naked maidens lilly white," ranged in a circle around
the three Graces; in the middle, set as "a precious gemme,"
is "another damzell," Colin's pastoral love.

> Looke how the Crowne, which *Ariadne* wore
>   Upon her yvory forehead that same day,
>   That *Theseus* her unto his bridale bore,
>   When the bold *Centaures* made that bloudy fray,
>   With the fierce *Lapithes*, which did them dismay;
>   Being now placed in the firmament,
>   Through the bright heaven doth her beams display,
>   And is unto the starres an ornament,
> Which round about her move in order excellent.

[54]

Such was the beauty of this goodly band,
  Whose sundry parts were here too long to tell:
  But she that in the midst of them did stand,
  Seem'd all the rest in beauty to excell,
  Crownd with a rosie girlond, that right well
  Did her beseeme. And ever, as the crew
  About her daunst, sweet flowres, that far did smell,
  And fragrant odours they uppon her threw;
But most of all, those three [Graces] did her with gifts endew.
                              (*FQ*, VI.x.13–14)

The description gathers its energy around the figure of the country maid, giving to both her garland and her person the marvelous ordering power of Ariadne's crown, which is encircled by the stars and surmounts the "bloudy fray" of Centaurs and "fierce Lapithes." The scene combines pastoral simplicity with all the dignity of the parallel to Ariadne; the extended simile not only specifies the maiden's power, but her beauty. Above all, the vision, with its flowers and gifts of the Graces, embodies to the watching Calidore the harmony he finds in his own pastoral love.

Even the briefest consideration of this scene reveals the strength and grace that Spenser finds in Calidore's retirement. Sidney's heroes do not have one moment so idyllic as this one. It is worth remembering that the *Arcadia* begins with a lament for the departure of Urania, the celestial Venus. When Pyrocles describes the beauty of Arcadia and imagines the goddess who must be at its center, Sidney finds it necessary to warn us of the disorder of his mind, his speech "dissolved in it selfe, as the vehemencie of the inwarde passion prevayled" (*F*, I.57). Spenser's hero is able to forget the burdens of conscience and to appreciate without conflict the proffered riches of leisure and love. When Calidore is actually in the pastoral world, he is fully given over to it; Spenser does not remind us forcefully of the requirements of heroic judgment. Only when Calidore returns to his quest does he attempt to put the pastoral episode into perspective:

> For all that hetherto hath long delayd
> This gentle knight, from sewing his first quest,
> Though out of course, yet hath not bene mis-sayd,
> To shew the courtesie by him profest,
> Even unto the lowest and the least.
>
> (*FQ,* VI.xii.2)

Pastorella turns out to be of gentle birth, and at the end of the book the country is viewed only as one of the places where, according to the scheme of the book, the hero can demonstrate his courtesy. However, like much of the excellent pastoral poetry of *The Faerie Queene*, the vision of the Graces has succeeded in teasing the reader away from the poem's heroic theme. The strengths of love are not necessarily the strengths of the active life.

In an eclogue placed late in the *Arcadia* (Book Three), Sidney imagines a pastoral episode that may further help to illustrate the nature of his difference from Spenser. This poem parallels the experience of Pyrocles and Musidorus in love and has special importance because it contains an unexpected personal reference to Sidney. In the revised version of the *Arcadia,* it appears as a dream of Amphialus, warrior cousin and unsuccessful suitor of Philoclea. However, the lady of the poem is named Mira, and the verses have been taken over without adaptation from a narrative that Sidney deleted from his revised version. Originally the song belonged to Philisides, pupil of "oulde Languette" (a reference to Hubert Languet, Sidney's continental mentor and friend); it tells of the "desperate worck of Fortune" by which this fictional Philip Sidney "was become a Shepehearde" (*F*, IV.320). In Samothea, the introductory prose tells us, Philisides was raised as a knight adept both in fighting and in study. He had traveled to ripen his judgment and, having returned home, "continewed to use the Benefites of a quyet mynde" until "Love . . . diverted this Course of Tranquility." The tale is a familiar one, but the fable in alexandrines that follows it has, if not striking verse, some striking details.

It begins as a dream vision, the dream of an untroubled mind "with freer wings of fleshly bondage free." The language is heavily salted with assurances of the hero's innocence of "those captiving snares / Which heav'nly purest gifts defile in muddy cares" (*Arc.* 73:17–18). In a forest of Samothea, he feeds on "Nature's sweet repast" and teaches his "healthfull senses" to know the gifts and beauties of nature:

> Those lampes of heav'nly fire to fixed motion bound,
> The ever-turning spheares, the never-moving ground;
> What essence dest'nie hath; if fortune be or no;
> Whence our immortall soules to mortall earth doo flowe.
>
> (*Arc.* 73:43–46)

Like Marvell's thoughtful pastoralist, he is to learn that "Two Paradises 'twere in one / To live in Paradise alone." His downfall begins with a breaking asunder of the moon and a noise that makes him think of Doomsday. From a chariot drawn by doves and sparrows, which has descended from the moon, emerge "two Ladies (Ladies sure / They seemed to me) on whom did waite a Virgin pure." The reader is put off balance in a way he should come to expect from Sidney; for the lady who appears to be Diana from her huntress' garb has a heavy pace and "meagre cheere," and Venus, whose doves we have recognized, has a "wanton woman's face." Only the attendant nymph Mira is attractive and to her description are given the most graceful lines of the poem: "But cald, she came apace; a pace wherein did move / The bande of beauties all, the little world of Love" (*Arc.* 73:89–90).

In the action that follows Sidney offers, as he did in *The*

Lady of May, a pastoral choice. Philisides is to assume the role of Paris, but we are reminded that his choice is more difficult than that of his classical model. Diana's beauty cannot be seen in a "face that shooke with spite," and Venus can only smile *"As though* she were the same, as when by *Paris'* doome / She had chiefe Goddesses in beautie overcome." As Diana explains it, Philisides must choose between her and Venus, one finally to have sovereignty over the other. Between the goddesses there had raged such fierce battles that "discord foule hath stain'd / Both our estates." She describes the destruction vividly: their temples have been defaced, their offerings spoiled, their thousand altars overturned in the dust. Mortals have forgotten their names. The lad of "spotlesse truth" must select the worthier of the two so that the goddesses can cease their struggles and renew their strength. They bind themselves by oath to his decision whatever it might be. However, they are outraged when he chooses neither of them, but rather Mira, whom we have known all along he regards as embodying "indeed a sweet consent / Of all those Graces' giftes." Though they must yield to his choice and bestow their powers on Mira, they also announce their revenge. Beauty, the gift of Venus, will rouse his desire, but Diana will secure the maid's chastity: "the chastnesse I will give / In ashes of despaire . . . shall make thee live." The goddesses depart, and the dreamer awakes trembling.

So this Elizabethan Paris receives the punishment of fire without even the fleeting rewards of a Helen's love. Philisides inherits for himself the wars of Venus and Diana, whose destructive power draws our attention away from the beauty of the young maid Mira. So satiric a view of the goddesses is characteristic of Sidney. They are aging beldames, Venus seen only in her wanton aspect as earthly desire and not in her exalted role as Platonic love. Sidney's verse also lacks the elevation of the Spenserian pastoral episode. Sidney reserves his Eden for the pleasures of Reason (and it is important to remember that those pleasures grow, for him, logically into heroic action); his fable casts strong doubts on the possibility of untroubled vision — even the momentary vision of Calidore or of the poet in Petrarch's sonnets — once one enters the world of love.

This fable, the dream of Philisides, dramatizes a fall away from the straightforward growth and positive values of the active life — a fall as real and inevitable as the greater Fall it parallels and parodies. The fall of Philisides, emblematic as well of the fate of Pyrocles and Musidorus, can be taken as a key to the *Arcadia*. In Sannazaro, the only fall is the fall from the grace of a lady; Sincero and his fellows are redeemed by poetry, by being gathered into the artifice of Arcadia. Sidney's *Arcadia* is concerned with something more complicated — the chaos of desire, the inroads of passion upon the heroic life, the struggle to regain lost reason through virtuous love. The poems of Sidney's work, like Sannazaro's, deal almost exclusively with love, but confusions and bafflements multiply rather than disappear when heroes enter the pastoral world.

THE ARCADIAN RHETORIC

S<small>IDNEY</small>'S "gallant variety" of verses in the *Arcadia* divides itself into two groups: eclogues and occasional pieces.[1] The eclogues are to be found clustered between books of the romance, four sets of them joining the five books that make up the *Arcadia*, and are thus distinguished from the occasional poems that are scattered singly through the text as part of the current of action. To the eclogues, Sidney allots a special function; there he draws most noticeably upon Sannazaro and the framework of the Italian *Arcadia*, presenting each set of eclogues as a dramatic unit on the model of the Italian pastoral.[2] The action of the romance halts; the Arcadian shepherds, who play virtually no role in the prose narrative, gather together; and the reader is suddenly transported into that timeless world in which sports, dancing, and poetic performance are the only valuable kinds of action. Sidney accepts Sannazaro's mise-en-scène as the natural refuge of the lover and as a landscape rich in inventions about love.

> But certainely, all the people of this countrie from high to lowe, is given to those sportes of the witte, so as you would wonder to heare how soone even children will beginne to versifie. Once, ordinary it is among the meanest sorte, to make Songes and Dialogues in meeter, either love whetting

their braine, or long peace having begun it, example and emulation amending it.   (*F*, I.27–28)

The ingenuity and variety of verse forms are striking, as they are in the Italian *Arcadia*. Here, in Sidney's eclogues, the experiments in Italian and classical meters for which he is noted are to be found.[3] But, given his view of love's corrosive effects upon the heroic life, Arcadian eclogues pose a further problem: to what extent can the exiled courtiers respond to the ideal landscape and richness of invention? how far can Arcadia temper their already painful experience of love?

1

Significantly, pastoral entertainment, which in Sannazaro's golden world is the order of the day, becomes in Sidney's Arcady a matter of interlude, of momentary felicity in performance. Before the First Eclogues the princesses, the queen Gynecia, and the disguised princes visit the scene chosen for the entertainment. We recognize the theater as Sannazaro's when we meet it in Sidney's stylized description:

> It was indeed a place of delight; for thorow the middest of it, there ran a sweete brooke, which did both hold the eye open with her azure streams, and yet seeke to close the eie with the purling noise it made upon the pibble stones it ran over: the field it self being set in some places with roses, and in al the rest constantly preserving a florishing greene; the Roses added such a ruddy shew unto it, as though the field were bashfull at his owne beautie: about it (as if it had bene to inclose a *Theater*) grew such a sort of trees, as eyther excellency of fruit, statelines of grouth, continuall greennes, or poeticall fancies have made at any time famous.
>
> (*F*, I.118–119)

Having savored the perfections of the setting, pointing to its particular harmony as a theater and as a scene worthy of "poeticall fancies," Sidney suddenly prods the reader to a consciousness of his use of convention. In rush a fierce lion and a bear; the disguised princes are immediately put on their mettle to defend Philoclea and Pamela. Sidney does not mean us to be frightened; the effect is to amuse us by setting one romantic device, the intruding beasts, against another, the perfect setting. But the intrusion does remind us that for the courtly figures the landscape of Sannazaro has only an illusory beauty and happiness. It develops that the king's rebellious sister, Cecropia, has set the animals loose. While the king continues his personal caprices, she is preparing a revolution. In its gentle way the episode figures forth the dangers of pastoral retirement and the special values of vigilance. Before the eclogues begin, we are asked to be alert and critical of the seductions of the conventional Arcadian landscape. Again, when the spell of the First Eclogues has ended — a considerable spell that has kept shepherds and courtiers together far into the night — the opening of Book Two presses the reader to re-evaluate the place of these pastimes in the lives of the heroes, the Arcadian princesses, and Basilius the king: "*In these pastorall* pastimes a great number of dayes were sent to follow their flying predecessours, while the cup of poison (which was deepely tasted of this noble companie) had left no sinewe of theirs without mortally searching into it" (*F*, I.145).

Sidney's ambiguous attitude toward pastoral performance (both its content and the literary form it takes) is one with his ambiguous attitude toward love. Such pleasures are apt to be brought to the bar of heroic responsibility and heroic virtue. Pastime, in the person of the Arcadian shepherds, only briefly assumes the foreground. Claiming precedence for music and love, they introduce the opening eclogues with a dance that "made a right picture of their chiefe god *Pan,* and his companions the *Satyres*." Their concluding couplet sets the tone of the eclogues: "As without breath, no pipe doth move, / No musike kindly without love." But pastoral diversion must ideally be judged against the life of action and right government. The participation of a king and princes in a pastoral celebration — their nobility tarnished somewhat by the fact of their retirement and their base disguises — sharply dramatizes Sidney's point of view. Like a later set of aristocrats in a later country paradise, that of Mansfield Park, the courtiers of Arcadia cannot join an entertainment with the innocence and impunity of shepherds.

Basilius, forgetful of his life as king to the point that he has come to live among the shepherds in their "desert places," becomes through this action both reprehensible and comic. As king of Arcadia, where even "the very shepheards have their fancies lifted to so high conceits," he has his choice of shepherd singers "either for goodnesse of voice, or pleasantnesse and wit." He encourages them by "great courtesie and liberalitie." But the grounds for criticizing his prolonged retirement to the forest lodges are clear. A loyal citizen, Kalander, defines the problem: "there is no cause to blame the Prince for somtimes hearing them; the blame-worthinesse is, that to heare them, he rather goes to solitarinesse, then makes them come to companie" (*F*, I.28). Poets are not to be banished from this commonwealth, as they are from Plato's ideal state. However, Basilius falls into the danger of solitariness, of only indulging his passions and his taste for passionate song. His behavior at the end of the First Eclogues is clownish rather than kingly: Zelmane, really Pyrocles in his Amazon guise, has just directed a song to the princess Philoclea with whom he is in love. Basilius, who has not penetrated the disguise and thinks Zelmane really a woman, imagining that the song was directed to him, falls to the ground in delight.

> What exclaiming praises *Basilius* gave to *Zelmanes* songe, any
> man may ghesse, that knowes love is better than a paire of
> spectacles to make every thing seeme greater, which is seene
> through it: . . . Yea, he fel prostrate on the ground, and
> thanked the Gods, they had preserved his life so long, as
> to heare the very musique they themselves used, in an earthly
> body.   (*F*, I.144)

Sidney's eclogues, then, are presented as a variety of court
masque, at which the king does not always behave as well as
he should. His disorder is surprising, a recognizable upsetting
of convention; for Basilius and his queen, the princesses and
the princely lovers (even though disguised) are expected to
maintain the courtly decorum that aristocrats do in a masque.

Though they participate in the pastoral revels, Pyrocles and
Musidorus are not absorbed into the shepherds' world as
easily as Sannazaro's hero is accommodated to Arcadia. Even
in a moment of relaxation, at an entertainment, Sidney does
not slacken his dramatic reins. The princes share the shepherds' skill in song; love haunts their minds and "waketh in
invention"; and like the shepherds they think of song as "a
more large expressing" of the passions (*F*, I.127). On the
other hand, the princes style themselves as lovers with "the
impediments of honor, and the torments of conscience."
These qualifications determine the special nature of their
poetry, as they attempt to translate the experience shared with
the shepherds into attitudes and language more appropriate
to their life of honor. They do not talk of the simple satis-
factions of fulfilled desire, but of the hazards of desire and of
that hoped-for state of virtuous love that informs the mind.
So Musidorus, now the shepherd Dorus, about to join in the
First Eclogues, rationalizes his delight in his new state: "more
proud of this estate, then of any kingdom: so manifest it is,
that the highest point outward things can bring one unto, is

the contentment of the mind: with which, no estate; without which, all estates be miserable" (*F*, I.116). But he registers as well the dangers they must undergo:

> O heaven and earth . . . to what a passe are our mindes brought, that from the right line of vertue, are wryed to these crooked shifts? But o Love, it is thou that doost it: thou changest name upon name; thou disguisest our bodies, and disfigurest our mindes. But in deed thou hast reason, for though the wayes be foule, the journeys end is most faire and honourable. (*F*, I.117)

In the eyes of Pyrocles and Musidorus, the pastoral state largely symbolizes "foule wayes"; it is a state to which they have been reduced and from which they may eventually be redeemed by the virtues of love.

It is necessary to point out the sharp distinction between courtiers and shepherds, a distinction not operative in Sannazaro's pastoral, in order to explain the interest of some otherwise dull poems, long pastorals, in the first two sets of eclogues. Cast as singing contests in either *terza rima* (the standard form of the Italian eclogue) or hexameters, these poems represent a strange breed of pastoral indeed — more "dramatic incidents" than "musical compositions," to adopt Ringler's useful distinction.[4] In the most significant of them, courtly speakers oppose Arcadian shepherds, using the form of the singing contest to present opposed views of love and to emphasize the rigorous immunity of the princes to simple pastoral happiness. The poems are exploratory in more than their attempt to hew English lines to the shapes of Latin hexameter and Italian triple rhyme. They express discomfort with aspects of the pastoral convention. They pose voices and attitudes against one another; they project courtly figures who self-consciously redefine the role of pastoral lover. Awkward as they are, the poems show Sidney's critical mind attempting to dramatize some "questions of love" and maintaining the hostility to *otium* displayed in *The Lady of May*.

In the poem that stands at the head of the First Eclogues, Lalus, a rustic, challenges Dorus, the disguised Musidorus. Their *terza rima* exchanges set up a clear, in fact schematic, contrast between the real shepherd and the disguised hero. The two speakers even invoke different muses: Lalus calls on Pan and favors plain speech; Dorus makes a "high attempt" and addresses a Muse whom he asks to "historifie" his mistress' praise. Lalus loves a country maid, Kala; Dorus cannot identify his mistress "whose name to name were high presumption." Kala can be described with homely simplicity and comic awkwardness:

> A heape of sweetes she is, where nothing spilled is;
> Who though she be no *Bee*, yet full of honie is:
> A *Lillie* field, with plowe of *Rose* which tilled is.
> Milde as a Lambe, more daintie than a Conie is:
> Her eyes my eyesight is, her conversation
> More gladde to me, then to a miser monie is.
>
> (*Arc.* 7:28–33)

Dorus' mistress defies description and can only be praised with elaborate (but not very readable) hyperbole:

> O happie Gods, which by inward assumption
> Enjoy her soule, in bodie's faire possession,
> And keep it joynde, fearing your seate's consumption.
> How oft with raine of teares skies make confession,
> Their dwellers rapt with sight of her perfection
> From heav'nly throne to her heav'n use digression?
>
> (*Arc.* 7:40–45)

Lalus is advised against love by a prattling father; Dorus, philosopher that he is, is warned by a personified and high-toned Reason against reaching "beyond humanitie" in his love. The poem experiments with the *sdrucciola* (triple

[66]

rhyme), but even in these experiments Sidney distinguishes his two speakers from one another: the real shepherd, as in the passage above, speaks in a base style depending on monosyllables (particularly the postponed verb, "is") for rhymes; Dorus, in keeping with the exalted state of his love, draws his rhymes from a ponderous Latin vocabulary ("consumption," "assumption," "confession," "digression").

It is easier to point out the intention of this poem — its attempt to contrast vocabularies of love — than it is to claim its success as a pastoral poem. In its intricate form the poem invites comparison with Sannazaro; metrically it follows the Italian's second eclogue very closely.[5] But Sidney's poem is much more abstract than Sannazaro's, and, as we might expect, the only hints of pastoral richness enter in the rustic's speech. Lalus, like the shepherd Espilus in *The Lady of May*, is intended as a figure of fun, boasting of his wealth in "many hundred sheep." Still he has a native sense of the fullness of pastoral love that is completely denied Dorus:

> . . . my sheep your foode shall breed,
> Their wooll your weede, I will you Musique yeeld
> In flowrie fielde; and as the day begins
> With twenty ginnes we will the small birds take,
> And pastimes make, as Nature things hath made.
> But when in shade we meet of mirtle bowes,
> Then Love allowes, our pleasures to enrich,
> The thought of which doth passe all worldly pelfe.
>
> *(Arc. 7:123–130)*

Dorus, who feels the "inward bondage" of heroic lovers, scorns this kind of felicity. In his reply he transforms Lalus' offerings one by one into an inner landscape of despair. He dramatizes the strength of his desires, the distance between him and his virtuous love, and the necessary degree of separation from pastoral happiness:

My foode is teares; my tunes waymenting yeeld:
Despaire my fielde; the flowers spirits' warrs:
My day newe cares; my ginnes my daily sight,
In which do light small birds of thoughts orethrowne:
My pastimes none: time passeth on my fall:
Nature made all, but me of dolours made:
I finde no shade, but where my Sunne doth burne:
No place to turne; without, within it fryes:
Nor helpe by life or death who living dyes.

(*Arc.* 7:138–146)

Insofar as there is any strength or vitality at all in Dorus'
poetry, it appears in lines like these, which express the destructive power of love. Dorus' despair in lines 135–146 rings
true. It succeeds poetically because of the sense of ceremony
in Sidney's use of the *frottola*, a verse form he adapts from
Sannazaro. Lacking end rhymes, the lines are connected by
a chain of interior rhymes that provide only muted accents;
a word at the center of each line echoes the concluding word
of the preceding line. The pattern emphasizes the short
clauses that make up the ritual denial of pastoral joys, while
continuing the flow of lament with as little break as possible.
Sidney parallels exactly the items that signify Lalus' sim-
plicities of desire (music, fields, flowers) in creating Dorus'
inner landscape. This landscape symbolizes Dorus' separation from simplicity, a separation enforced by his sense of
"thoughts orethrowne," his "pastimes none." What Sidney
is trying to find for his lovers of high conscience is a ceremony
marking their despair, their separateness from the familiar
ceremonial felicity of the Arcadian setting inherited from
Sannazaro.

From this point of view, another of the eclogues (*Arc.* 13)
deserves attention.[6] Here the two princes, "desiring in a
secret maner to speake of their cases" so that the princesses
may understand who they really are, rather self-consciously

discuss pastoral disguise and pastoral song. The exchange, potentially a witty one, is twisted out of shape in an effort to produce English quantitative verse. (Significantly these "dignified" attempts at domesticating Latin meters are reserved for the princes, denied to shepherds.) Each prince — Musidorus dressed as a shepherd, Pyrocles as an Amazon — points out the advantages of the other's state. Pyrocles–Zelmane envies the directness of lament available to the shepherd Dorus; Dorus replies that his suffering does not diminish "when trees daunce to the pype, and swift streames stay by the musicke." Dorus is jealous of the heroic appearance of Zelmane, who can openly act out her virtue; Zelmane counters that heroic virtue is dwarfed by the powerful effects of love. If heroic virtue cannot lighten the pains of love,

> Then do I thinke in deed, that better it is to be private
> In sorrows torments, then, tyed to the pompes of a pallace,
> Nurse inwarde maladyes, which have not scope to be breath'd out.
>
> (*Arc.* 13:102–104)

And so pastoral lament is to be preferred, its virtue being that it is "not limited to a whispringe note, the Lament of a Courtier."

To express the immediate destructive power of love, the princes must find emblems for that power in the pastoral landscape around them:

> And when I meete these trees, in the earth's faire lyvery clothed,
> Ease I do feele (such ease as falls to one wholy diseased)
> For that I finde in them parte of my estate represented.
> *Lawrell* shews what I seeke, by the Mirre is show'd how I seeke it,
> Olive paintes me the peace that I must aspire to by conquest:
> *Mirtle* makes my request, my request is crown'd with a willowe.
> *Cyprus* promiseth helpe, but a helpe where comes no recomforte.
> Sweete Juniper saith this, thoh I burne, yet I burne in a sweete fire.

Ewe doth make me be thinke what kind of bow the boy holdeth
Which shootes strongly without any noyse and deadly without smarte.
Firr trees great and greene, fixt on a hye hill but a barrein,
Lyke to my noble thoughtes, still new, well plac'd, to me fruteles.

(Arc. 13:113–124)

The verse, characterized by abstract pastoral equations, continues, using the trees of the forest one by one to "tell" the lover's sorrows. Awkward by any standards, the poem is interesting for the amount of maneuvering it goes through, for its deliberate discussion of what constitutes high lament. The poetic strand seized is that of pastoral melancholy, a strain familiar enough in Sannazaro and in his Petrarchan models. But Sidney expresses the desolate qualities of pastoral exile almost abstractly. Like Dorus' complaint in the opening eclogue — though in less skillful verse — the poem inventories the lover's sorrows relentlessly, using items of the pastoral landscape as emblems. The habit of listing (carried here to an absurd extreme), of assigning an emotional equivalent to every pastoral landmark ("Despaire my fielde; the flowers spirits' warrs"), gives to Sidney's pastoral love poems their peculiarly insistent quality, their sense of inescapable pain. A lyric like Dorus' "My sheepe are thoughts" enlists the same responses — a hyperconsciousness of how the pastoral mode can be made to symbolize the sufferings of the courtly lover: "My sheepehooke is wanne hope, which all upholdes:/ My weedes, Desire, cut out in endlesse foldes" (*Arc.* 17).

The effect such poems give is one of an unyielding spareness. And Sidney rarely dramatizes the other side of pastoral experience: the richness for the Petrarchan lover in his new life of isolation or the satisfaction felt by Sannazaro's lovers in becoming part of the world of Arcadian imagination. We may remember Petrarch's pastoral lines, the vision to be balanced against the lover's desolate mountain wanderings:

I' l'ho più volte (or chi fia che m'il creda?)
ne l'acqua chiara e sopra l'erba verde
veduto viva, e nel troncon d'un faggio,
e'n bianca nube sì fatta che Leda
avria ben detto che sua figlia perde,
come stella che'l sol copre col raggio.

(Rime, 129)

The only characters in Sidney's eclogues who sense the richness of pastoral love denied to Dorus and Zelmane are the shepherds. They have the Third Eclogues to themselves and act out a rustic wedding completed by an epithalamium.[7] Sidney admires their simplicity but, ultimately treating them with comic irony, reminds us that they are incapable of the higher ranges of feeling that characterize his heroes. The best known lyric from the *Arcadia,* "My true love hath my hart, and I have his," celebrates simple felicity in love. One of the surprises for the reader of the *Arcadia* is the frame in which Sidney places this song about the exchange of hearts. Dorus devises a plan to deceive Miso, wife of the king's clownish servant Dametas. He angers her by imagining a scene in which Dametas is found dallying with a beautiful shepherdess. The frail beauty of the fictional shepherdess' song, "My true love hath my hart," lasts for a moment and is ironically qualified by its connection with the deception of the gross Miso and her boorish husband.

2

Of the unrelenting spare quality of Sidney's pastoral laments there is no better example than the double sestina, "Yee Gote-heard Gods." It makes a virtue of the unflinching abstraction that characterizes the laments of Pyrocles and Musidorus. Although the double sestina is not sung by the Greek princes, it too is designed to illuminate their situation.

Sidney assigns the poem to Strephon and Klaius, two mysterious shepherds who play roles of varying importance in the different versions of the romance. As originally presented in the unrevised *Arcadia*, they appear in the Fourth Eclogues: "two gentlemen they were, bothe in Love with one Mayde in that Contry named *Urania* thought a Shepherdes Daughter, but in deede of farr greater byrthe" (*F*, IV.307). Like Musidorus they have disguised themselves as shepherds in order to serve a lady, and the double sestina they sing is filled with a sense, shared by the Arcadian heroes, of the destructive power of love.[8] In the revised version of 1590, Strephon and Klaius assume more prominent roles. They open the romance and, rescuing Musidorus from a shipwreck, introduce the hero into Arcadia. They are no longer described as gentlemen in disguise, but as shepherds capable of the highest ranges of feeling. The only shepherds not native to Arcadia, they are clearly to be distinguished from the rustics of the eclogues. They have come to the seacoast to mourn the departure of Urania for the island of "Cithera." In Klaius' praise of her we get a measure of what has been lost to the shepherds:

> But in deede as wee can better consider the sunnes beautie, by marking how he guildes these waters, and mountaines then by looking upon his owne face, too glorious for our weake eyes: so it may be our conceits (not able to beare her sun-stayning excellencie) will better way it by her workes upon some meaner subject employed. And alas, who can better witness that then we, whose experience is grounded upon feeling? hath not the onely love of her made us (being silly ignorant shepheards) raise up our thoughts above the ordinary levell of the worlde, so as great clearkes do not disdaine our conference? hath not the desire to seeme worthie in her eyes made us when others were sleeping, to sit vewing the course of heavens? when others were running at base, to runne over learned writings? when other marke their sheepe, we to marke our selves? hath not shee throwne reason upon our desires, and, as it were given

eyes unto *Cupid*? hath in any, but in her, love-fellowship maintained friendship betweene rivals, and beautie taught the beholders chastitie?　　　　　　　　　　　　　　(*F*, I.7–8)

Urania embodies love, Neoplatonic felicity; through her, passion is purified. Klaius' lament implies that, with her departure, Arcadia has fallen back upon the mercies of a blind Cupid, back into what Musidorus termed the "foule wayes" of love. The lost harmony for which these shepherds mourn means to them what the sense of wholeness in love means to Pyrocles and Musidorus. We cannot be sure of the way in which Sidney might have worked out the roles of Strephon and Klaius in a fully revised *Arcadia*, but it is clear from the two existing versions that their experience parallels the heroes' separateness from the felicitous Arcadian setting; for that reason they are allowed to sound the opening notes of the *Arcadia*. We hear their particular tone in the verse of the double sestina, which, for purposes of analysis, is quoted in full:

STREPHON:
Yee Gote-heard Gods, that love the grassie mountaines,
　　Yee Nimphes which haunt the springs in pleasant vallies,
　　Ye Satyrs joyde with free and quiet forrests,
　　Vouchsafe your silent eares to playning musique,
　　Which to my woes gives still an early morning:
　　And drawes the dolor on till wery evening.

KLAIUS:
O *Mercurie,* foregoer to the evening,
　　O heavenlie huntresse of the savage mountaines,
　　O lovelie starre, entitled of the morning,
　　While that my voice doth fill these wofull vallies,
　　Vouchsafe your silent eares to plaining musique,
　　Which oft hath *Echo* tir'd in secrete forrests.

S:　I that was once free-burges of the forrests,
　　Where shade from Sunne, and sporte I sought in evening,
　　I that was once esteem'd for pleasant musique,

Am banisht now among the monstrous mountaines
Of huge despaire, and foule affliction's vallies,
Am growne a shrich-owle to my selfe each morning.

K: I that was once delighted every morning,
Hunting the wilde inhabiters of forrests,
I that was once the musique of these vallies,
So darkened am, that all my day is evening,
Hart-broken so, that molehilles seeme high mountaines,
And fill the vales with cries in steed of musique.

S: Long since alas, my deadly Swannish musique
Hath made it selfe a crier of the morning,
And hath with wailing strength clim'd highest mountaines:
Long since my thoughts more desert be then forrests:
Long since I see my joyes come to their evening,
And state throwen downe to over-troden vallies.

K: Long since the happie dwellers of these vallies,
Have praide me leave my strange exclaiming musique,
Which troubles their daye's worke, and joyes of evening:
Long since I hate the night, more hate the morning:
Long since my thoughts chase me like beasts in forrests,
And make me wish my selfe layd under mountaines.

S: Me seemes I see the high and stately mountaines,
Transforme themselves to lowe dejected vallies:
Me seemes I heare in these ill-changed forrests,
The Nightingales doo learne of Owles their musique:
Me seemes I feele the comfort of the morning
Turnde to the mortall serene of an evening.

K: Me seemes I see a filthie clowdie evening ,
As soon as Sunne begins to clime the mountaines:
Me seemes I feele a noysome sent, the morning
When I doo smell the flowers of these vallies:
Me seemes I heare, when I doo heare sweete musique,
The dreadfull cries of murdred men in forrests.

S: I wish to fire the trees of all these forrests;
I give the Sunne a last farewell each evening;
I curse the fidling finders out of Musicke:
With envie I doo hate the loftie mountaines;
And with despite despise the humble vallies:
I doo detest night, evening, day, and morning.

[74]

K: Curse to my selfe my prayer is, the morning:
  My fire is more, then can be made with forrests;
  My state more base, then are the basest vallies:
  I wish no evenings more to see, each evening;
  Shamed I hate my selfe-in sight of mountaines,
  And stoppe mine eares, lest I growe mad with Musicke.

S: For she, whose parts maintainde a perfect musique,
  Whose beawties shin'de more then the blushing morning,
  Who much did passe in state the stately mountaines,
  In straightnes past the Cedars of the forrests,
  Hath cast me, wretch, into eternall evening,
  By taking her two Sunnes from these darke vallies.

K: For she, with whom compar'd, the Alpes are vallies,
  She, whose lest word brings from the spheares their musique,
  At whose approach the Sunne rase in the evening,
  Who, where she went, bare in her forhead morning,
  Is gone, is gone from these our spoyled forrests,
  Turning to desarts our best pastur'de mountaines.

S: These mountaines witnesse shall, so shall these vallies,
K: These forrests eke, made wretched by our musique.
  Our morning hymne this is, and song at evening.

(Arc. 71)

Lovers like these have haunted literature at least since Petrarch's poet entered his enclosed valley that symbolized the confines of the lover's state. The reader recognizes Petrarch's figure reborn in Sannazaro's double sestina:

> Lasso, ch'io non so ben l'ora nè 'l giorno,
>   che fui rinchiuso in questa alpestra valle;
>   nè mi ricordo mai correr per campi
>   libero o sciolto . . .

These once-free shepherds who find the pastoral world no more than a prison reappear in Sidney's poem:

> I that was once free-burges of the forrests,
>
>   . . . . .
>
> Am banisht now among the monstrous mountaines
> Of huge despaire, and foule affliction's vallies.

It was Sannazaro, as we have seen, who realized that the very form of the double sestina could signify the unavoidable pains of love in the pastoral world. His terminations — *rime, pianto, giorno, campi, sassi, valle* — mark the limits of the lovers' experience. In the repetitions and returns of these words, Logisto and Elpino come against the confines of place (fields, rocks, valley), of time (the recurring days), and of their own endless laments (songs and complaints). The world of Strephon and Klaius in Sidney's poem is defined by similarly recurring words. As William Empson's excellent reading puts it:

> [The poem] beats, however rich its orchestration, with a wailing and immovable monotony, for ever upon the same doors in vain. *Mountaines, vallies, forrests; musique, evening, morning*; it is at these words only that Klaius and Strephon pause in their cries; these words circumscribe their world; these are the bones of their situation; and in tracing their lovelorn pastoral tedium through thirteen repetitions . . . we seem to extract all the meaning possible from these notions.[9]

Sidney's handling of these repetitions is much more adventurous than Sannazaro's, more original and complicated, more sensitive to proliferating meanings. Empson summarizes the associations that each of the six terminating words has gathered by the time the poem has made its returns. To take one as an illustration:

> *Mountaines* are haunts of Pan for lust and Diana for chastity, to both of these the lovers appeal; they suggest being shut in, or banishment; impossibility and impotence, or difficulty and achievement; greatness that may be envied or may be felt as your own (so as to make you feel helpless, or feel powerful); they give you the peace, or the despair, of the grave; they are the distant things behind which the sun rises and sets, the too near things which shut in your valley; deserted wastes, and the ample pastures to which you drive up the cattle for the summer.[10]

Yet it is necessary to understand not only the range of emotions included, but also the way in which these associations gather in time, the way they are disposed in the muted crescendo of the poem. This is what really distinguishes Sidney's poem from Sannazaro's and makes it such a splendid example of the individual talent working with tradition. Sidney has seen the possibilities in Sannazaro's organization of the sestina as a dialogue, employing pairs of stanzas, statement and response. But in Sidney's poem the shifts in attitude from one pair of stanzas to the next mark the stages in a magnificent crescendo that is absent in its Italian model. The poem moves from an opening memory of past joys through a violent climax of despair in the stanzas beginning, "I wish to fire the trees of all these forrests"; it closes with a brief coda of recollected harmony. Strephon and Klaius move away from the ordinary experience of pastoral joys, transforming them ever more rapidly into symbols of desire and suffering. There is no better example of the abstract quality of Sidney's pastoral than the continuing reminders in this poem that objects in the pastoral world are merely emblems for the flailing imagination of the despairing lovers. In Sannazaro's poem, the reader accepts fields, rocks, and valleys as emblems of the lovers' imprisonment simply because they recur twelve times, used in their literal meanings, and in their repeated cycles create a sense of confinement. But Sidney makes their symbolic value explicit almost from the outset, identifying his landscape as "monstrous mountaines / Of huge despaire, and foule affliction's vallies." From then on, these landmarks of time and place shift rapidly, assuming in each stanza a different metaphorical role — sometimes simply equated with mental states ("my thoughts more desert be then forrests"); sometimes caught in the act of being changed by the singer's tortured mind

("Me seems I see the high and stately mountaines, / Transforme themselves to lowe dejected vallies").

These nightmares are all the more convincing because
they develop before the reader's eyes. The opening pair of
stanzas sets a tone of ceremony and concord, which serves
as a measure for the departures that follow. Strephon calls
upon the gods of the earth — "Gote-heard Gods," nymphs,
and satyrs — and Klaius, the gods of the heavens — Mercury,
Diana, and Venus. Between them their invocations sanctify
both the pastoral landscape, with its welcoming "grassie
mountaines," "pleasant vallies," and "free and quiet forrests," and the comforting order of time, with the evening
heralded by Mercury, the moon represented by Diana, and
the morning led in by Venus. Here we have only a hint of
the inner state of the lovers that separates them from the
harmony around them. Nature in its innocence and variety
contains the contraries of "pleasant vallies" and "savage
mountaines," Diana and "Gote-heard Gods"; only the lovers'
discord invites the tedium of a day measured by woes from
"early morning" to "wery evening."

In the second pair of stanzas we move to the lovers themselves, to their recollections, with Strephon's "I that was
once free-burges of the forrests" and Klaius' "I that was once
delighted every morning." The shift is interesting. Not only
does it introduce a different relationship between speaker
and landscape, but it brings the six key words into differing
kinetic relationships. "Mountaines" and "forrests," in the
first section part of the same orderly exterior landscape, are
here opposed to one another. This second pair of stanzas
poises the lovers' former state as free hunters and musicians
in tune with these valleys against their present inward feelings of banishment and darkness. With the only enjambment of the poem, we move decisively from the free outer

landscape of the past, the hunters' forests, to the confining inner landscape of the present: "Am banisht now among the monstrous mountaines / Of huge despaire, and foule affliction's vallies." Mountains now symbolize despair and are monstrous rather than grassy. Strephon's once pleasant music now makes him a "shrich-owle" to himself each morning. Stable elements in the landscape lose their sure value so that molehills seem mountains to Klaius; they are replaced in his mind, as music is by cries.

This pair of stanzas, like every pair but the fifth, maintains a rigid grammatical parallelism: "I that was once (line 1) . . . I that was once (line 3)." Shifts of grammatical structure occur between pairs, but not within them. These structural repetitions, operating independently of the recurring key words, measure the pace of the poem and preserve the ceremonial quality of the opening invocations. Like the simple and occasionally colloquial diction, these effects control and mute the growing violence of the poem, a violence that begins to be felt in surreal phrases like "Am growne a shrich-owle to my selfe each morning."

As the poem progresses, then, elements of landscape take their places metaphorically as part of the inner world of fancy and lose their status as solid objects. Recollection continues in the third pair of stanzas with much less sense of the normal round of pastoral life that the shepherds have left behind. We hear briefly of "happie dwellers of these vallies," of "their daye's worke, and joyes of evening." But Strephon's "deadly Swannish musique" has "with wailing strength clim'd highest mountaines," and he finds his "state throwen downe to over-troden vallies." The metamorphosis of "forrests" in these two stanzas shows most graphically how recurring key words lead us into new areas of experience. For both Strephon and Klaius, the word becomes part of the lover's characterization of his thoughts, but the repetition introduces complexity rather than simplicity. Strephon declares, "Long since my thoughts more desert be then forrests," and Klaius responds, "Long since my thoughts chase me like beasts in forrests." Meanings proliferate. Thoughts are wastelands not rich and growing like forests; if we remember the "hurtlesse trees" of *The Lady of May*, we understand the state from which the lover has fallen. Thoughts are also active and pursue Klaius inescapably like savage beasts. Here Sidney not only characterizes a mental state, but refers ironically to the physical freedom of the earlier section of the poem: "I that was once delighted every morning, / Hunting the wilde inhabiters of forrests." The hunter becomes the hunted, the forest a place of danger.

The double sestina grows more energetic as it becomes more despairing. At the center of the poem, the cycle of rhymes beginning once more, the narration moves into the present tense. The juxtaposition of "sweete musique" and "murdred men in forrests" announces a climax of special ferocity. Now (lines 49–60) the feeling that the opening benevolent landscape has become, to the mind, a prison reaches its height. The verbs are active — not simply the seeing, feeling, and hearing of the previous set of stanzas, but gestures of violence toward the pastoral world: "I wish to fire the trees of all these forrests"; "I curse the fidling finders out of Musicke." Rhythm is accelerated, and each line is a completed sentence and action, contrasting with the longer sentences of earlier stanzas. Forests, evening, music, mountains, valleys, morning: each of these fixed points becomes in Strephon's verses a time or place to be destroyed. At the climax, Sidney breaks the rigid parallelism enforced upon every preceding pair of stanzas. Strephon's speech displays more violence than Klaius': "I wish to fire; I curse; I doo hate." Klaius' answer recognizes that violent gestures are futile, recoil, and cannot satisfy: "My fire is more, then can be made with forrests." He turns the violence upon himself: "I wish no evenings more to see, each evening." He catalogues his humiliations ("My state more base, then are the basest vallies") and concludes with a fierce recognition of his isolation even from the ceremonies of the poem: "And stoppe mine eares, lest I growe mad with Musicke."

At this point Sidney turns dramatically to introduce the cause of the shepherds' savage despair, the departure of Urania. It is a brilliant stroke, taking advantage of the sestina form in which the last word of a stanza is repeated to conclude the opening line of the next. The form poises Klaius' height of distress, "lest I growe mad with Musicke," against the wholesome power of Urania, "she, whose parts maintainde a perfect musique." In the metamorphosis of one word's meaning, in the swift traverse of emotional territory from music that maddens to music that signifies perfection, effect and cause are brought together and the progress of the poem recalled for us. The last pair of stanzas is a coda of recollected harmony; Urania embodies the order with which the poem began. Her departure spoils the forests and turns mountains to deserts. After the poem's note of despair, the reader is ready to believe that Urania does induce in her beholders liberty and awe, that she illuminates nature so as to make it seem ceremonious. Yet it is difficult to agree with Theodore Spencer that this ending relieves the despair of the poem.[11] Rather, the expansiveness of these last lines would seem to confirm it, emphasizing the gap between felicitous past and present distress. Each repeating word reminds us of the beauty of a world the shepherds have renounced, and the very structure of these last stanzas reminds us of the contrast: each stanza begins with a four-line praise of Urania but returns, with the main verbs that have been postponed to the fifth line, to the singers' distress, to the "eternall evening," the "spoyled forrests," the deserts and dark valleys of the body of the poem. We never learn why Urania has left Arcadia, but it appears to be a condition of Sidney's poetic interest that the fallen state is the present state, that the vision of wholeness and innocence has been shattered for these lovers.

One of Sidney's metaphors for Urania's power is that she "in straightnes past the Cedars of the forrests." It recalls the innocence and singleness of the forester's life in *The Lady of May*: "O sweet contentation to see the long life of the hurtlesse trees." In love, as well as in the active life, he is able to envision a state of perfection. But it is striking that he should describe this contentment in love from a distance, as a remote vision. He sees its perfections in memory, but imagination cannot effectively relieve the vivid sufferings and unresolved desires of the present. He lingers over, indeed fiercely celebrates, the consequences of this fallen state. This special feeling on Sidney's part is, I believe, the reason for the poem's distinctive power, its growing intensity. He did not find such strength in Sannazaro or in any of his predecessors in the double sestina.

To see this poem alongside the double sestina of Sannazaro is instructive. Both poems register a sense of hopeless imprisonment and banishment in nature. But halfway through his poem, Sannazaro introduces a voice heard by Elpino, which promises him (for no good reason) more fortunate days. He falls back upon the powers of poetry and announces that, like Orpheus, he will make woods and rocks dance and doves sing every day. This is enough to resolve the immediate problems of desire, and Elpino shifts to a more comfortable poetic mode in the second half of the poem without any apparent dramatic justification. Sidney accepts no such resolution; he sustains his sense of dramatic propriety so that when, in the last two stanzas, a shift in tone occurs, it comes as a felt necessity, as a tribute to the order that no longer exists. Orphic powers do not suffice: "And stoppe mine eares, lest I growe mad with Musicke."

What is sacrificed by Sidney, of course, is the high Arcadian mode, the celebration of harmony in love that exists as part of Petrarch's vision and dominates Sannazaro's. Sidney chooses to emphasize the dark melancholic vein in the pastoral lament. We may remember that, when Petrarch speaks of pastoral exile, it is to balance the rich possibilities of imagination in solitude against the pains of deprivation and desire. Petrarchan love is a continuous process of weighing and experiencing these two sets of feelings; it brings into play both the richness and the barrenness of pastoral. In Sannazaro's *Arcadia*, the rewards of imagination and the influx of poetic powers harmonize and obscure the lover's suffering. What we remember most from Sidney is the forceful imagery, the nightmare quality of "the dreadfull cries of murdred men in forrests," "the mortall serene of an evening," and "the Nightingales doo learne of Owles their musique."

Sidney's poem must be taken, I think, as a criticism of the easy resolutions of Sannazaro's *Arcadia*, and it should give us some indication of why the pastoral sections of the English romance strike a reader so often as un-Arcadian. The same poetic sensibility that lies behind Astrophel's sudden cry, "'But, ah,' Desire still cries, 'give me some food,'" is at work in the poet's dealing with the operatic lovers of Sannazaro's world.

3

The double sestina differs from Sidney's shorter poems in degree rather than in kind; its strength in organizing repetitions, the recurring words and grammatical structures, is in fact the strength of the occasional poems of the *Arcadia*, though none of them is as impressive as Strephon and Klaius' massive eclogue. What Empson says of the double sestina can be applied to the songs and sonnets of the romance: "It is seldom that the meaning of a poet's words is built up so flatly and steadily in the course of using them. And limited as this form may be, the capacity to accept a limitation so unflinchingly, the capacity even to conceive so large a form as a unit of sustained feeling, is one that has been lost since that age." [12] The remark about sustained feeling and largeness of form is, of course, applicable only to the double sestina. But the notion of severe limitation of poetic resources is a generally fruitful one for considering Sidney's poems. What Empson terms "flatness" results from Sidney's low-keyed vocabulary, his use of monosyllables, and his reliance on rhythm, grammar, and devices of repetition rather than on highly allusive metaphor. As if the double sestina did not have enough of its own built-in repetitions, Sidney introduces further repeating schemes — anaphora and the rigidly parallel stanzas — not demanded by the form. It is true, of course, that in the double sestina he also draws upon powerful imagery, upon the vivid and haunting quality of certain expressions in combination with the strict formalities of the verse. The other Arcadian poems rely less on imagery; it is no wonder that critics of form like Roman Jakobson can cite them as splendid examples of the "poetry of grammar." [13]

For Sidney's contemporaries they constituted a poetry of rhetoric as well. That curious manual, *The Arcadian Rhetorike* of Abraham Fraunce, quotes from the double sestina at the conclusion of a catalogue of rhetorical figures, "sith all [its] grace and delicacie proceedeth from the figures aforenamed." [14] Fraunce has been discussing the repetition of words and sounds, figures belonging properly to the training of the orator [15] — yet he is concerned with the vitality of these rhetorical patterns in poetry. He takes delight in pointing out the combination of strictly poetic devices of repetition with the recognized rhetorical devices; rhyme, stanza, and meter assume places beside epizeuxis, anadiplosis, anaphora, and the other exotic capitals of the rhetorician's world. There is a strong emphasis, in other words, on the way in which the very structure of verse takes on the force of persuasive figures. *The Arcadian Rhetorike* collects its examples from Homer, Virgil, Petrarch, and Tasso, but draws most noticeably upon Sidney's *Arcadia,* using poems still unpublished when Fraunce's book appeared in 1588. Compiled by a member of the Sidney circle, this handbook of poetic persuasion ranks high the elaborate symmetry of form that we have come to recognize as a feature of Sidney's verse in the *Arcadia.*[16]

To the modern reader, indeed to the post-Shakespearean reader, the occasional poems of the *Arcadia* must seem bare — depending for their effect as they do, far more on rhetorical urgency than on metaphorical complexity. These poems, found in the body of the romance rather than among the eclogues, lament the overthrow of reason by love; they are spoken by the courtly figures of the romance who are caught in the strong toils of desire. In most of these verses Sidney places patterns of repetition at the service of wit, of the neat assurance that the experience of love, however chaotic for his characters, has been accepted as inevitable. Such lovers are masters of their griefs; if they do not often achieve Petrarch's lyric visions of perfection in love, they can at least measure the effects of love upon their own minds and register the dilemmas of their fallen states. Here is Pyrocles—

Zelmane, loved by those he does not love and loving a princess who does not love him:

> Loved I am, and yet complaine of Love:
> As loving not, accus'd, in Love I die.
> When pittie most I crave, I cruell prove:
> Still seeking Love, love found as much I flie.

(Arc. 20)

The tone of dignity, fostered by balanced lines and recurrent words, lends an appearance of ordered judgment to an otherwise irrational and painful situation: that of the pursuer pursued. Repetitions confirm the speaker's frustration (loved, he complains of love); by the end of these four lines, the word seems empty of any hope it may have held for him. Yet the epigrammatic form offers us assurance that this is what courtiers must expect when they give way to their passions.

Patterned rhetorical devices are used in other ways to characterize the lover's experience: for example, to express succinctly the recoil of the passions. Gynecia at one point takes "a right measure of her present mind." She speaks of the way love and jealousy "their strengthes together tie": "Love wakes the jealous eye least thence it moves: / The jealous eye, the more it lookes, it loves" (*F*, I.310). The couplet describes an unbreakable circle of desire and affection. The two actors, personified love and the jealous eye, act upon each other: love, which begins in independent action as subject and actor of the first line, ends entwined with jealousy; as predicate of the second line, "loves" becomes the intensified action of the jealous eye that Love had awakened.

The singleness of effect that characterizes the short lyrics of the *Arcadia* can best be discussed by examining a complete poem. The following verses are written on a sandy bank

near a stream, one of the resorts of the ever-complaining
Zelmane–Pyrocles:

> Over these brookes trusting to ease mine eyes,
> (Mine eyes even great in labour with their teares)
> I layde my face; my face wherein there lyes
> Clusters of clowdes, which no Sunne ever cleares.
>> In watry glasse my watrie eyes I see:
>> Sorrowes ill easde, where sorrowes painted be.
>
> My thoughts imprisonde in my secreat woes,
> With flamie breathe doo issue oft in sound:
> The sound to this strange aier no sooner goes,
> But that it dooth with *Echoe's* force rebound
>> And make me heare the plaints I would refraine:
>> Thus outward helps my inward griefes maintaine.
>
> Now in this sande I would discharge my minde,
> And cast from me part of my burdnous cares:
> And in the sandes my paynes foretolde I finde,
> And see therein how well the writer fares.
>> Since streame, aier, sand, mine eyes and eares conspire:
>> What hope to quench, where each thing blowes the fire?
>
>> *(Arc.* 21)

These lines make their impression through the cumula-
tive power of repeating figures and stanzas; the poem is
diffuse rather than concentrated in its local effects. Verbs
are not heavily charged with metaphorical meaning, and
Sidney often uses the weaker auxiliary forms ("doo issue,"
"would refraine"). Nor are his few metaphors particularly
striking. The poem is stretched to a simple and well-defined
framework. In each of the three stanzas, the lover looks to
some aspect of nature around him for "ease." But in the
stream he sees his own reflection and tears; in the air he
hears his complaint echoed; and in the sand he sees the
verses he has just written, the poem we have just read. The

poem's form emphasizes once more the unbreakable circle of desire. The last couplet recapitulates its orderly progress ("streame, aier, sand") and reminds us that the poem's logic is emblematic of the inescapable suffering of Pyrocles. In the background of the poem, the four elements are in play: the lover's fire unsolaced by the water, air, or earth around him.[17] They serve as a subdued reminder of the perfect natural order from which, as in the double sestina, the lover has separated himself. Behind the poem lies the assumption that sometime in the past the speaker might have been able to find comfort in recognizing the order of nature ("trusting to ease mine eyes"). In his present fallen state, he is relentlessly cut off even from Sannazaro's consolation, nature's harmony reflected in a well-sung lament.

At least in theme and in the related rigor of its structure, the poem resembles the double sestina; but of course its tone is lighter, less tragic. Because it is less spectacular, less rich, we can see more of Sidney's poetic scaffolding. A skillful single tone of address disciplines the poem; individual figures are marshaled quietly and assuredly toward a limited and well-defined end. The first stanza is built upon recurrent phrases: "to ease mine eyes, / (Mine eyes even great in labour"; "my face; my face wherein there lyes / Clusters of clowdes." Fraunce cites this stanza in *The Arcadian Rhetorike* as an example of the figure anadiplosis.[18] These repetitions gently draw our attention away from the gesture of seeking consolation ("trusting to ease mine eyes . . . I layde my face . . .") to the speaker's inner disorder, which, ironically, prevents him from being comforted. Instead of the natural clouds mirrored in the stream, he sees his own face. In Sidney's *Arcadia* there are no "outward helps" for the relaxed will. The carefully balanced couplet that concludes the stanza neatly summarizes the dilemma: "In watry glasse my watrie eyes I see: / Sorrowes ill easde, where sorrowes painted be." The caesura in each line is heavily marked after the fourth syllable, and in each line the divided halves mirror one another in imitation of the action of the stanza. The elegant concluding turn restores bite to the conventional conceit of lovers reminded of their tearful state by brooks and streams.

Rhetorical turns, less frequent, organize the rest of the poem. The second stanza takes up the repeated "sound" of lines 8 and 9 in the rhyming "rebound" of line 10, all these effects pointing up the "echoes" around which the stanza is built. The summarizing couplet of the stanza again opposes "outward helps" to "inward griefes." It would be foolish to overstress the skill of this poem, one of many such small and quiet successes in the *Arcadia*. Much of the reader's pleasure comes from piecing out its ground plan and discovering the energy of mind that Sidney applied to rhetorical schemes in poetry. Such patterns suggest an inescapable logic of the emotions, conveyed in a manner both worldly and decorous, which invigorates the conventional conceits and dramatic situations of pastoral love poetry. The poems, spoken by voices acquainted with the arts of persuasion, wryly and reasonably show us what happens when reason is overcome.

Most of the short pieces of the *Arcadia* are sonnets, and Sidney manages to adapt the sonnet form to his own insistent Arcadian rhetoric. The sonnets of the first two books of the romance follow the form used by Surrey — the form later to be Shakespeare's — ABAB/CDCD/EFEF/GG. Surrey makes of this open form a line-by-line accounting. The sestet of his sonnet in praise of Geraldine illustrates the point:

> Honsdon did first present her to mine yien:
> Bright is her hewe, and Geraldine she hight.
> Hampton me taught to wishe her first for mine:
> And Windsor, alas, dothe chase me from her sight.
> Her beauty of kind her vertues from above.
> Happy is he, that can obtaine her love.[19]

Another sonnet, "How each thing save the lover in spring reviveth to pleasure," again catalogues his experience line by line:

> When Windsor walles susteyned my wearied arme,
> My hande my chin, to ease my restlesse hed:
> The pleasant plot revested green with warme,
> The blossomd bowes with lusty Ver yspred,
> The flowred meades, the wedded birdes so late
> Mine eyes discover: and to my mynde resorte
> The ioly woes, the hatelesse shorte debate,
> The rakehell lyfe that longes to loves disporte.[20]

Neither Surrey nor Sidney (in these Arcadian sonnets) has a very clear notion of the sestet as a unit of development, with power to move the sonnet forward or change its course. It required Shakespeare's mastery of the open Surrey form to realize that possibility. But Sidney does see in the loose rhyme scheme opportunities for more than Surrey's descriptive catalogues. He chooses the repeating quatrains as his unit of expression. Here is a lament sung by the disguised Pyrocles:

> In vaine, mine Eyes, you labour to amende
> With flowing teares your fault of hasty sight:
> Since to my hart her shape you so did sende;
> That her I see, though you did lose your light.
>
> In vaine, my Hart, now you with sight are burnd,
> With sighes you seeke to coole your hotte desire:
> Since sighes (into mine inward fornace turnd)
> For bellowes serve to kindle more the fire.

Reason, in vaine (now you have lost my hart)
My head you seeke, as to your strongest forte:
Since there mine eyes have played so false a parte,
That to your strength your foes have sure resorte.
   And since in vaine I find were all my strife,
   To this strange death I vainely yeeld my life.

(*Arc.* 14)

This sonnet does not differ in pattern from the longer lyric, "Over these brookes trusting to ease mine eyes." In effect it falls into three stanzas, each roughly parallel in content and form, followed by a summarizing couplet. Here is a poem in which the mind measures its fall. Sidney's material is the psychology of love: hasty sight admits the lady's image to Pyrocles' heart, and reason despite itself is overthrown. Each stanza addresses a different faculty ("In vaine, mine Eyes"; "In vaine, my Hart"; "Reason, in vaine"). In the final couplet, the "I" of the poem makes his appearance to assess the accumulated frustration.

Like "Over these brookes," this sonnet describes in its progress a circle. The lover in his audit turns from eyes and vain tears to the heart where the true, the inner, vision of his mistress can be found. In the second stanza we learn that the heart's "vision" brings, instead of Platonic illumination, desire and sighs. Pyrocles' concern is not with his mistress' perfection, but with his own loss of control. In the third quatrain, reason, which once ruled his heart, retreats to the head, its "strongest forte," only to discover the traitor eyes in command. Reason can find no place then in the lover's world. One falls from grace because of the action of the senses, and the process is made a continuous one in this sonnet.

To accent the orderly progress of personified faculties (eyes-heart; heart; reason-heart-eyes), Sidney employs a set of tight grammatical parallels. Each stanza falls into the pattern "In vaine . . . since" (with an inversion in line 9 postponing the appearance of "in vaine"). The words are resumed deliberately in the couplet: "And since in vaine I find were all my strife / To this strange death I vainely yeeld my life." The repetition is particularly effective as part of the witty and concise couplet that, in both lines, marks the caesura after the fourth syllable; the rhyming half of each line is a clause beginning with "I." It is the expectation set up by the recurring "vain" ticking away through the poem and now repeated in the coda that is responsible for the real bite of the poem. "Vainely," interposed between the familiar Petrarchan contraries of life and death in love, gives an unexpected fillip to that opposition. For "vain" connotes throughout the entire poem — as it does in line 13 — the speaker's fruitless attempts to resist passion; now at the end of the sonnet he recognizes, with wry wit, that accepting passion is also vain and self-defeating, hence a "strange death." This shift of attitude tests our alertness and, of course, succeeds because it mocks expectations prepared by the rigid parallelism that precedes it.

To realize how important the rhetorical structure of this poem is, we need only survey its conceits. Sighs as bellows to fan the fires of love, living death, love as a combat of reason and passion: these are well-worn conceits with subdued and merely local importance. The rhetorical structure does not serve a dominant metaphor, as it frequently does in the sonnets of Petrarch and Shakespeare. What sting the poem conveys comes from a rhetorical surprise, the repeated "vainely" of its last line.

The Arcadian laments are designed to strike off a single impression. If a reader were confronted with a mixed bag of sonnets from the *Arcadia* and *Astrophel and Stella* and had no clues from the content of the poem, in most cases he could identify the Arcadian poems from their intentionally static quality. Of eighteen sonnets in the romance, fourteen are organized on the scheme of closely related quatrains, involving repeated figures or words, and a summarizing couplet. Sometimes the quatrains, to obtain a more subdued effect, repeat their rhymes, as in the case of a sonnet in Book Three, "Aurora now thou shewst thy blushing light" (*Arc.* 56). The rhyme scheme, ABAB/ABAB/ABAB/CC, heightens the impression of monotonous and inescapable pain that the poem urges upon the reader. Sidney achieves something of the effect of the double sestina by using only four rhyme words in the quatrains (*light, bait, right,* and *wait*), employing a different meaning for each word as it is repeated in each stanza. The couplet repeats the word *show*, first using it as a verb and then as a noun.

Sidney carries the technique of close repetition to an extreme in two poems of Book Three. One of them employs a series of fourteen words rhyming with *bright (Arc.* 42). Another, a lament of Zelmane's welcoming the cave as refuge for her "stormy rage of passions darcke" (*Arc.* 39), uses only *light* and *dark* as its rhymes. The poem consists of the familiar series of parallel stanzas deploying its rhymes ABAB/BABA/ABAB/AB and postponing the main clause until the final couplet has been reached: "I like this place, wheare at the least the darke / May keepe my thoughtes, from thought of wonted light." This sonnet, though it lacks the excitement of much of Sidney's other verse, is an interesting and revealing exercise. In it we glimpse the bare bones of the sonnet as used schematically in the *Arcadia*; it appears intentional that repeating structures assume a symbolic value of their own. Here the dilemma of the heroic lover — his yearnings for "reasons light" or for the purity of "beauties light," which are blocked by "passions darcke" — is signified by the ceaseless alternation between *light* and *dark* in the rhymes of the poem.

Yet it would be unfair to overstress the uniform conception of the Arcadian sonnets. Especially in Book Three, Sidney sets the sonnet to tasks different from those already described. For the first time he gives independent attention to the sestet,[21] allowing it to convey a shift of meaning or interest. Although it is impossible to date these sonnets in relation to one another or to the sonnets in *Astrophel and Stella*, the poems that open Book Three represent a more adventurous view of the possibilities of the sonnet than one finds in the poems of the earlier books.[22] They seem to represent new discoveries about the form for Sidney. A modest example is Philoclea's impatient sonnet, an address to time in the hope that she will soon be united with Pyrocles:

> O stealing time the subject of delaie,
> (Delay, the racke of unrefrain'd desire)
> What strange dessein hast thou my hopes to staie,
> My hopes which do but to mine owne aspire?
>
> Mine owne? o word on whose sweete sound doth pray
> My greedy soule, with gripe of inward fire:
> Thy title great, I justlie chalenge may,
> Since in such phrase his faith he did attire.
>
> O time, become the chariot of my joyes:
> As thou drawest on, so let my blisse draw neere.
> Each moment lost, part of my hap destroyes:
>
> Thou art the father of occasion deare:
> Joyne with thy sonne, to ease my long annoys.
> In speedie helpe, thanke worthie frends appeare.

> (*Arc.* 53)

This sonnet reveals the pressure of a mind in motion in a way that sets it apart from the earlier static sonnets of lamentation. Something has happened between the irritation of the opening of the octet ("O stealing time the subject of delaie") and the assured wish that opens the sestet ("O time, become the chariot of my joyes"). Philoclea, beginning with a series of cautious repetitions ("delaie / Delay"; "my hopes . . . / My hopes"; "mine owne . . . / Mine owne?"), takes on confidence in the second quatrain, reminding herself of her lover's faith. The joyful cajolery of the sestet is the result. The shift in tone from octet to sestet allows us to see time from two angles, first as the "subject of delaie," then with the anticipation of "chariot of my joyes." Sidney uses the sonnet in this case as something more than a series of repeating quatrains.

One of the later sonnets in Book Three moves even further from Sidney's version of the Surrey sonnet. This sonnet rhymes ABBA/ABBA/CDE/CDE, adopting the interlocking Italian form. It is also the first of the *Arcadia*'s sonnets to rely completely upon feminine rhymes. More important, it treats love and desire in more complex fashion than some of the earlier poems do. The speaker is Basilius, deceived into thinking he has spent a night of pleasure with Zelmane, when actually he has been with his own wife Gynecia:

> O Night, the ease of care, the pledge of pleasure,
> Desire's best meane, harvest of hartes affected,
> The seate of peace, the throne which is erected
> Of humane life to be the quiet measure,
>
> Be victor still of *Phoebus*' golden treasure:
> Who hath our sight with too much sight infected,
> Whose light is cause we have our lives neglected
> Turning all nature's course to selfe displeasure.
>
> These stately starrs in their now shining faces,
> With sinlesse sleepe, and silence, wisdome's mother,
> Witnesse his wrong which by thy helpe is eased:

Thou arte therefore of these our desart places
The sure refuge, by thee and by no other
My soule is bliste, sence joyde, and fortune raysed.

(*Arc.* 69)

The sonnet would be remarkable if only for its masterly invocation of Night, which later becomes almost a formula in Elizabethan poetry: the successive alliterative epithets for sleep and night convey in somnolent rhythms a sense of welcome repose. What is remarkable in Sidney's treatment is the manner in which the second quatrain qualifies the experience of the first. Night is not only the "ease of care," but "Desire's best meane." He can characterize it as part of the natural order, "harvest of hartes affected," in the sense that night satisfies desire, the inevitable product of the day. But desire also breaks nature's course, causing "lives neglected" and "selfe displeasure." The poem while offering respite keeps the speaker aware of "desart places," of which Strephon and Klaius constantly remind us. The rhetorical trick of the poem is to blame the day and Phoebus for the speaker's guilt; but that guilt remains, in the intrusive and striking "desart places," part of Basilius' sense of his situation. For such balance of the worlds of peace and desire in Sidney's poetry, we look usually to the more complicated verse of *Astrophel and Stella*.

But it is true that the dominant poetic mode of the *Arcadia* is the static, plangent lament spoken by characters of high breeding, mourning over desire. Though the later poems of the *Arcadia* reveal new freedom and complexity in Sidney's handling of the resources of the sonnet, the range of the Arcadian sonnets is narrow, their function in the romance a limited one. Tragic lament is only one way to register the chaos of desire in a long work that has other ways of gaining the same effect — comic disguises, dramatic adventures, and maneuvers of plot. One of the great changes we shall see in *Astrophel and Stella* is that more pressure is put on the verse; love's complications are revealed not in a mosaic of poetry and plotted prose, but in the turnings of individual poems and a sequence of sonnets.

4

The love poems of the *Arcadia* refer the reader implicitly to the standards of the heroic world; they dramatize the lover's abdication of reason and the attempt to find order in love. It remains to ask what resolution, if any, Sidney effects between the destructive passion expressed in these lyrics and the behavior originally demanded of Pyrocles and Musidorus by their heroic education. We know that such a resolution does not occur in the poetry of the *Arcadia*, and now we must refer to the prose for a further definition of Sidney's position.

One clue to Sidney's attitude toward the relation of love and duty lies in the series of tales in Book Two. These can be understood as an extended comment on the central action in Arcadia. Almost every one of the episodes deals with lust or an excess of love. Most important, these tales link private excess with public destruction in the same way that, in the Arcadian section, Basilius' lust is part of the lack of control that leads to the Arcadian rebellion and makes possible Cecropia's plots against the state. For example, Erona, the queen of Lycia, having ordered the images of Cupid pulled down, is suddenly seized with love for Antiphilus, a commoner. He marries her and, as king, becomes a prey to flatterers, making "his kingdome a Teniscourt" (*F*, I.330). His eventual scorn of Erona and pursuit of Artaxia, the queen of Armenia, leads to his own death and to Erona's imprisonment. In a parallel tale, the king of Iberia marries a townsman's wife, Andromana, former mistress of his son Plangus. She directs her efforts toward forcing the uxorious king to banish his son and to give her effectual rule over Iberia. She tries also to seduce Pyrocles and Musidorus and, failing, makes every effort to take revenge on them.

It is one of the many calculated ironies of the carefully constructed second book of the *Arcadia* that the principal royal families involved are related to one another [23] and that the violence, both public and private, works itself out in the deaths of the innocent heirs, Palladius and Zelmane. Palladius, the son of Andromana and the king of Iberia, loses his life at the hands of Andromana's own soldiers while helping Pyrocles and Musidorus to flee the country. Zelmane, disguised as a page, dies of grief from the accumulated treacheries of her father Plexirtus and from unrequited love for Pyrocles.

Sidney's most moving dramatization of the public violence that can spring from personal passions comes in his description of a crucial battle in Amphialus' defense of Cecropia's castle. Amphialus has led his troops into a dangerous position after several skirmishes that were destructive for both the Basilian forces and his own. He has lost any sense of responsibility toward his followers in the hope that he can win glory for himself and hence gain the love of Philoclea. His love for her, the reader knows, will never be returned.

> And now the often-changing Fortune began also to chaunge the hewe of the battailes. For at the first, though it were terrible, yet Terror was deckt so bravelie with rich furniture, guilte swords, shining armours, pleasant pensils, that the eye with delight had scarce leasure to be afraide: But now all universally defiled with dust, bloud, broken armours, mangled bodies, tooke away the maske, and sette foorth Horror in his owne horrible manner. But neither could danger be dreadfull

to *Amphialus*-his undismayable courage, nor yet seem ougly
to him, whose truely-affected minde, did still paint it over with
the beautie of *Philoclea*.   (*F*, I.392–393)

It is all there: the very real courage of Amphialus, the
power of love to paint over the scene with glories, but also
the waste of riches, the violence that misdirected action and
excess of love can bring. With a slow turn of the kaleido-
scope, the whole scene takes on a new and horrible com-
plexion; his vision clouded by passion, Amphialus misuses
his own instinct for heroism and martial virtue.

If the central action in Arcadia has anything in common
with the heroic flashbacks of Book Two, it is a recognition
of the degree to which feelings of love threaten or under-
mine the heroic life. Yet Sidney seems of two minds in his
presentation of the princes' stay in Arcadia. Love, when
disciplined, understood, and directed, can be the strongest
ally of the heroic life. The Arcadian episode with its leisure
for love can be important; the trials of love can be for
Pyrocles and Musidorus part of the larger experience of
learning to judge and act. Ideally, as Strephon and Klaius
know, love can lead to thoughts "above the ordinary levell of
the worlde" by beginning with "experience . . . grounded
upon feeling." But in a fallen world — and of this condition
Sidney keeps reminding us — even the most innocent love
has its admixture of passion. This is the plight of Sidney's
Astrophel, and it is also the situation of Pyrocles and Musidorus.

If there is any criticism to be made of the ending of the
Arcadia, it must be made with the full realization that
Sidney did not have the opportunity to revise his romance
beyond Book Three. Even so, one wonders what sort of
resolution would have been possible. What seems to be
missing is the kind of climactic episode that one finds par-

ticularly in Book One of *The Faerie Queene*. If the princes have indeed had an education in the passions and been finally led back to the heroic world, one would like a demonstration of the harmony of the worlds of heroism and love, an episode that exemplifies the new fullness of knowledge in action.

However, this harmony of love and action is one of which Sidney himself was never certain. When at the end of the *Arcadia* Euarchus restores order, he judges that the princes, in abducting the princesses and in leaving the heroic world to adopt disguises, have abandoned the high standard of reason in action that is the ideal basis of Sidney's romance. Euarchus himself demonstrates the noble standards of the heroic world by refusing to withdraw his decision, even under the emotional stress of learning that the condemned heroes are his own son and nephew.

> If rightly I have judged, then rightly I have judged myne own children. Unlesse the name of a child, should have force to change the never changing justice. No no *Pyrocles* and *Musidorus* I prefer you much before my life, but I prefer Justice as far before you, while you did like your selves, my body should willingly have ben your shield, but I cannot keep you from the effects of your own doing. *(F, II.201)*

However, the awakening of Basilius dispels the tragic atmosphere, and the princes are free to go with their loves into the world of governors and heroes. Harmony comes as a result of comic accident.

For Sidney, then, there does not seem to be a final resolution of action and love. A description of both worlds — the world of responsible action and the world of pastoral love — is necessary for an adequate presentation of experience. There is no question of choosing "the quiet, retired life of the shepherd" as opposed to "chivalric and honorable achievement." [24] At the center of both worlds is imperfect man, attempting to exercise the obligations of reason. Sidney's heroic world offers the model of reasonable activity; his pastoral world presents in the vicissitudes of love a heightened example of the unavoidable obstacles to heroic striving.

PART TWO

ASTROPHEL AND STELLA

4

THE PETRARCHAN VISION

Love's not so pure, and abstract, as they use
To say, which have no Mistresse but their Muse,
But as all else, being elemented too,
Love sometimes would contemplate, sometimes do.
John Donne, "Loves Growth"

TEMPUS ADEST PLAUSUS AUREA POMPA VENIT. So Nashe heralded *Astrophel and Stella* upon its first edition, an unauthorized publication of 1591.[1] The golden procession proves to be a somewhat angular and witty set of one hundred and eight sonnets and eleven songs, and its richness lies not in the brocaded texture of particular poems, but in the fertility of invention that Sidney sustains over the entire set. Here, for the first time in English poetry, an engaging persona governs a whole sequence in the way that the lover of Laura controls with recognizable voice and attitudes the *Rime* of Petrarch. Whatever the biographical significance of *Astrophel and Stella*, it holds its rewards for the reader as a poetic sequence. Enough attention has been paid to the deduced narrative of Sir Philip Sidney's love for Penelope Rich,[2] but not nearly enough to the poetic enrichment given the simple ground bass of event.[3] Though a narrative is closer to the surface of Sidney's sequence than it is in most others, this narrative is composed of familiar elements: the knight taken by love, kept at a distance by his lady, allowed a kiss, finally separated from her and left complaining fiercely of love. It is the passions engaged by this narrative, the lover's reaction to it, that mark these sonnets as unique. Here, as in the *Arcadia*, we find a sharply defined concern for the corrosive effects of love upon the heroic life and the education of a Renaissance hero. The sonnet sequence allows Sidney to dramatize from yet another point of view the lofty aims of the lover and the defeats imposed by desire.

In the *Arcadia* the havoc of desire led to the comic game of disguises, to the ridiculous postures of the irresponsible Basilius, as well as to the nightmares of Strephon and Klaius. These comic and tragic insights are combined in the dramatic reactions of Astrophel. He stands apart as one of the most self-conscious of Elizabethan poet-lovers — a Protean figure by comparison with the heroes of the *Arcadia*. He is nothing if not critical of the way in which others have expressed their experience of love, of poets who trade in "poore Petrarch's long deceased woes." [4] Yet our ordinary terms, Petrarchan and anti-Petrarchan, are too crude to describe the nimble movements of Astrophel's mind. It is easy enough to see what is anti-Petrarchan in Shakespeare's "My mistress' eyes are nothing like the sun" or Sidney's own mockery of the Petrarchan in phrases like "living deaths, deare wounds, faire stormes, and freesing fires" (*AS*, 6). In each case the writer of the sonnet finds conventional hyperboles or Petrarchan oxymorons inadequate to the true voice of feeling. But Astrophel, in a more harmonious mood, invokes the Petrarchan contraries himself:

> Soule's joy, bend not those morning starres from me,
> Where Vertue is made strong by Beautie's might,

Where *Love* is chastnesse, Paine doth learne delight,
And Humblenesse growes one with Majestie.

(AS, 48)

Astrophel's opposing attitudes — his alternate mockery and acceptance of Petrarchan rhetoric — prevent us from making any simple decisions about his role in the sonnet cycle of which he is the protagonist. He seems to be calling attention to his own shifting attitudes more explicitly than one expects in a conventional Petrarchan cycle. He belongs among those lovers who not only suffer but, apprenticed in the rhetoric of love, are also acutely conscious of the role a lover is expected to play. When reading *Astrophel and Stella*, it is well to keep in mind the tragicomic experience of a later young Elizabethan hero:

> *Troilus*: O, let my lady apprehend no fear. In all Cupid's pageant there is presented no monster.
> *Cressida*: Nor nothing monstrous neither?
> *Troilus*: Nothing but our undertakings when we vow to weep seas, live in fire, eat rocks, tame tigers, thinking it harder for our mistress to devise imposition enough than for us to undergo any difficulty imposed. This is the monstruosity in love, lady, that the will is infinite and the execution confin'd, that the desire is boundless and the act a slave to limit.
>
> (III.ii.68–77)

The boundless desires and expectations of wonder embodied in Petrarchan rhetoric help to define the speech and character of both Troilus and Astrophel. Troilus accepts their promise naively. For him the marvels of love create a confusion of spirit and sense: "I am giddy; expectation whirls me round. / Th' imaginary relish is so sweet / That it enchants my sense." For Astrophel the promised refinements of love remain clear as a background against which he can test his own experience — his responsibilities to the heroic life or the strength of sexual desire. Often things are quite different from what he has been led to expect: he does not love at first sight (sonnet 2); he is impatient with attitudes his role imposes (sonnet 56: "Fy schoole of Patience, Fy, your lesson is / Far far too long to learne it without booke"). Petrarchan language comes to these young heroes as might the Ciceronian style,[5] as part of an inherited way of dealing with or projecting experience. Their characters are created for us in terms of their reactions to the language of the conventional lover, the degree to which they accept or resist it as a way of describing experience, the degree to which they exaggerate certain features of conventional language at the expense of others.

Petrarch again provides a beginning for our study. In what way do his sonnets furnish a meaningful framework for the discussion of Sidney's poems? What are some of the assumptions that lie behind the Petrarchan style? There is more to it than hyperbole and oxymoron, its most obvious and easily imitated features. With more precise knowledge about the resources of the convention, it will be possible to understand the special demands placed upon it by the protagonist of *Astrophel and Stella*.

1

Petrarch's songs and sonnets are designed to represent a lifetime of passionate attention to one mistress, to Laura. Their qualities of sustained devotion and acceptance of pain are truly remarkable, especially when we place them beside the energetic and impatient utterances of Astrophel. Never is there a question of the promise of Laura's favors,[6] as there is of Stella's in Sidney's sequence. An Italian critic has pointed out — without deprecation — that the strength of the *Rime* lies in their quality of *monotonia*; they strike a single note and focus with variations on a single emotional experience.[7] The satisfactory activity in Petrarch's poems is memory; pleasure lies in recalling the sudden illumination of his first sight of Laura. To that experience he returns again and again, and he pays tribute to its informing power by marking, year by year, the anniversary of the day on which it occurred. The poet's first vision of Laura (a point observed in Chapter One in another connection) becomes for him a type of the imagination of earthly beauty and an unfailing source of poetic invention. He willingly takes on symbolic exile ("In una valle chiusa d'ogn'intorno") and a painful separation from Laura, attempting to preserve in the mind's eye the wonder and fear of these first moments:

> Ivi non donne, ma fontane e sassi,
> e l'imagine trovo di quel giorno
> che'l pensier mio figura, ovunque io sguardo.
>
> *(Rime,* 116)

When it is accepted, such exile is quite literally the death of the lover, although it may be the birth of the poet. The *Rime* refract the poet's viewpoint from many angles; the balance of poetic emphasis constantly shifts back and forth, now stressing the fearful exhaustion, the painful frustration of separation from Laura, now responding to the enrichment of imagination in meeting her again or remembering the first encounter. But, in any case, recollection is at the center of these poems.

It is most important to emphasize the dramatic ground of the lover's trials: the series of dazzling presentations of Laura that recur frequently and justify the poet's sustained passion. Perhaps the most famous of these scenes is one based upon the appearance of Venus in Book One of the *Aeneid*:

Erano i capei d'oro a l'aura sparsi
  che'n mille dolci nodi gli avolgea,
  e'l vago lume oltra misura ardea
  di quei begli occhi, ch'or ne son sì scarsi.
e'l viso di pietosi color farsi,
  non so se vero o falso, mi parea:
  l' che l'ésca amorosa al petto avea,
  qual meraviglia se di subito arsi?
Non era l'andar suo cosa mortale,
  ma d'angelica forma, e le parole
  sonavan altro che pur voce umana;
uno spirto celeste, un vivo sole
  fu quel ch'i' vidi; e se non fosse or tale,
  piaga per allentar d'arco non sana.*

                                              (*Rime*, 90)

After a simple heralding *erano*, the initial impression of
the sonnet is that of brilliance: a figure suddenly appears,
golden hair loosened in the wind, eyes shining. The poem
gathers its first effects from these few striking details and
from the felicitous recall of Venus appearing, dressed as a
huntress, before Aeneas: "dederatque comam diffundere
ventis, / nuda genu nodoque sinus collecta fluentis" (and
she had given her hair to the winds to scatter; her knees
bare, and her flowing robes gathered in a knot).[8] The notion
of a miracle is introduced quietly and almost ironically in
the second quatrain when the poet describes the effect of
the vision; it is *no* miracle, he says, that one should be fired
by such a sight, by the look of pity he reads into her expres-

---

* Her golden hair was loosened to the breeze, which tangled it into a
thousand sweet knots; and the fine light burned beyond measure in those
beautiful eyes, where now it seldom shows. And her face took on pitying
colors, it seemed to me; I do not know whether true or false. I — who had
love's tinder in my breast — what wonder if it flared at once? Her movement was not a mortal thing, but that of an angelic form; and her words
sounded different from a mere human voice. A divine spirit, a living sun,
was what I saw, and if it is not so now, the wound does not heal though the
bow is slackened

sion. In the sestet the poem moves away from particulars to dramatize the fullness of his reaction. He shares some of the wonder of Aeneas' response to Venus, "o dea certe!" and closely echoes the Latin ("nec vox hominem sonat," line 328) in "le parole / sonavan altro che pur voce umana." To that vision of a pagan goddess, he adds the spendor of "angelica forma." The sestet is indeed a marvelously managed transformation building through negatives — what Laura was not ("Non era l'andar suo cosa mortale"; "altro che pur voce umana") — to the simple climax, what she was, achieved in a line of lovely balance: "uno spirto celeste, un vivo sole."

Only when we reach the last lines of the poem do we become fully aware that the narrative has been conveyed in past tenses. With a subtle modulation we move from the climax of "vivo sole" to the past definite, "fu quel ch'i' vidi," and a moment that we have been experiencing in the continuous past ("era," "sonavan") recedes before our eyes into the remote, the historical, the not-to-be-repeated. We have been blinded to the progress of time by the immediacy of Petrarch's vision. The poem is deftly arranged so that we should not be reminded until the end, though it prepares for the possibility that Laura may not be now as she was then ("se non fosse or tale") in a modifying phrase easily passed over in the first reading: in the opening quatrain, with an intrusion in the present tense, he remarks on the diminished brilliance of her eyes ("ch'or ne son sì scarsi"). The last lines of the sonnet bring together the present, with the possibility of a Laura touched by age, and the past with its fierce and lasting illumination. Laura may no longer be beautiful; but the wound does not heal though the bow is slackened. For a moment the lover's suffering, prominent in most of the poems but subdued here, comes to the surface with a reminder of the wound and the huntress. Yet the subject of the sonnet is really the vividness of memory and imagination.[9] The sonnet holds a number of contrary emotions in equilibrium: desire, at once painful and enchanting; the sense that beauty fades; and a feeling for the enduring mythical qualities of beauty. It is memory that resolves the conflicting elements; with its retrospective point of view, imagination is capable of restoring a moment of ideal beauty otherwise threatened by time and desire.

"Erano i capei" reveals an aspect of Petrarch's style more difficult to imitate than the oxymorons, the contraries of "dear wounds" and "living deaths" that became common currency for those who took the *Rime* as their model. In some of his best sonnets, Petrarch presents harmonious visions of Laura that yoke oppositions of feeling irrevocably and without violence. Such power is at work in a poem more "conventionally" Petrarchan than sonnet 90:

> In qual parte del ciel, in quale idea
> era l'esempio, onde Natura tolse
> quel bel viso leggiadro, in ch'ella volse
> mostrar qua giù quanto lassù potea?
> Qual ninfa in fonti, in selve mai qual dea,
> chiome d'oro sì fino a l'aura sciolse?
> quando un cor tante in sé vertuti accolse?
> benché la somma è di mia morte rea.
> Per divina bellezza indarno mira
> chi gli occhi de costei già mai non vide
> come soavemente ella gli gira;
> non sa come Amor sana, e come ancide,
> chi non sa come dolce ella sospira,
> e come dolce parla, e dolce ride.*

(*Rime*, 159)

* In what part of heaven, in what idea was the model from which Nature took that lovely glad face, in which it wanted to show, here below, how much it could do above? What nymph in a fountain, in the woods what goddess, ever loosened to the breeze such fine golden hair? When did a heart gather

This sonnet exemplifies a poise and maturity in the *Rime*, an acceptance of the lover's plight for the sake of the few moments of illumination and felicitous memory that form part of his experience. The poem reconciles opposing effects of love: its power to wound and to heal (lines 8 and 12). But what is uniquely Petrarchan about it is the resolving agent, the tone of wonder captured in the three rhetorical questions of the octet. These questions serve as hyperbolical praise of Laura: in what part of heaven, in what "idea" could Nature have found a model for Laura? What nymph, what goddess loosens to the breeze such fine golden hair? When did a heart hold so many virtues? She gathers to herself the brilliance of a nymph, a pagan goddess, and a divine beauty whose divinity (the poem leaves it unspecified) may derive from the realm of Platonic ideas or Christian virtue or some fusion of both. The transfiguring process is assisted by a pattern of repetitions, phrases echoing and reinforcing the questions asked: "in qual parte . . . in quale idea"; "Qual ninfa . . . qual dea." The poet's "death" is reserved for a qualifying clause ("benché la somma è di mia morte rea"), and the poem slips immediately into the tone of renewed admiration in the sestet. Discord reappears, reminding us of line 8, with "non sa come Amor sana, e come ancide." Then conflict is muted once more; for it is a privilege to know how Love wounds, a special knowledge conveyed by Laura's sweet speech and laughter. Any paraphrase obscures the rhetorical effectiveness of the three "dolce"s and the repeated "non sa come . . . e come . . . / chi non sa come dolce . . . / e come dolce." The rhetorical

---

so many virtues into itself? although their sum is guilty of my death. He looks in vain for divine beauty who never saw the eyes of this lady as she gently turns them; he does not know how Love heals, and how it kills, who does not know how sweetly she sighs, and how sweetly she talks, and sweetly laughs.

pattern and the unusually close rhyme of the sestet (CDCDCD) emphasize a bit of grammatical sorcery: *come* in line 12 connotes the "manner in which" — the manner in which love heals, the manner in which it kills; but in lines 13 and 14 *come* is an adverb intensifying *dolce*. It is a subtle shift, but of course all the sting of "come ancide" disappears when the adverb is subsumed in the echoing rhythms of "come dolce ella sospira, / e come dolce parla, e dolce ride." The human details of these last lines are given, by the pattern of the verse, something like the transcendent qualities of the vision in the octet; we feel this even before we recognize the special classical resonance of the last line, an echo, in the manner of the allusion to Virgil in "Erano i capei," of the Horatian "dulce ridentem Lalagen amabo, / dulce loquentem." [10]

Like "Erano i capei," this sonnet presents Laura in resplendent fashion. It illustrates another quality of Petrarch's style that goes along with such a presentation: his majestic public manner. The invitation to public admiration of Laura is a corollary of her uniqueness; she embodies a general truth that all should join the poet in recognizing. From the poet's recognition springs the grandeur and generosity of the rhetorical questions in the octet and the general claims in the sestet ("he who . . ."). The certainty and conviction that lie behind this sort of utterance should be remembered when we compare the *Rime* with some of the sonnets in *Astrophel and Stella*.

It would be a misrepresentation of the *Rime* to give the impression that all the poems convey brilliant visions of Laura, or indeed that all the poems so successfully harmonize pain and delight. But there are enough such presentations of her throughout Petrarch's collection to lend credibility and unity to the poet's rendering of experience: the long passion, the endless complaints, the yearly celebrations of their first meeting, the repeated enshrinement of places Laura has visited. The sonnets and canzoni evidence a continuing nourishment of the imagination, "emotion recollected in tranquility," and the source of such nourishment lies finally in the image, the heightened intuition of Laura's beauty, rather than in the changing, aging woman. Part of the assurance that lies behind the poems of wonder and public praise grows from Petrarch's insight into the nature of love poetry. He perceives that the apparently static relation between poet-lover and mistress is really a product of tension and poise. There are repeated dangers: chief among them, the ferocity of desire and the depredations of time. Only by re-creating his vision in the poems themselves is he able to preserve its initial fullness, its informing power. Petrarch's insight has its mythological buttress in the tale of Apollo and Daphne that threads through the *Rime*. His puns on the laurel and Laura justify themselves when he recognizes, in the sonnets, that only the poetic metamorphosis can preserve the beauty he has seen in the meetings that have roused his desire.

Such knowledge, hard-won, can be held in verse. Petrarch maintains a delicate balance between day-to-day passions and an evaluation that we might call, too simply, philosophical. The vitality of love poetry depends upon its power to meditate between, and in some cases fuse, momentary passionate attention and ideas, perhaps illusory, of permanence and value. It is well to remember Petrarch's own response to a charge made by his friend Colonna that Laura was *literally* a poetic fiction and a symbol for the Muse:

> You actually say that I have invented the name of "Laura" in order to have some one to talk about, and in order to set people talking about me, but that, in reality, I have no "Laura"

in mind, except that poetical laurel to which I have aspired, as
my long and unwearied toil bears witness; . . . On this point
would that your jests were true; O that it were dissimula-
tion and not madness.[11]

Presumably there are other — and less harmonious — relationships between the poetical passion and the human one
than that finally achieved by Petrarch in the *Rime*.

2

By emphasizing the dramatic function of the presentations
of Laura in Petrarch's sequence, I have wanted to call attention to some of the special qualities of Petrarch's style and
to some of the assumptions behind it. It is misleading to
claim, as Richard B. Young does, that by the end of Sidney's
sequence "Astrophel has been made aware of the nature of
Love as the Petrarchan universal."[12] Such a statement turns
Petrarchanism into a formula and ignores it as the product
of a highly individual poetic sensibility. Young is making
a valuable point about Sidney, however: that he uses elements of Petrarch's style more frequently than his opening
protestations of independence might suggest. But there are
as many varieties of Petrarchan style as there are good poets
who have found some meaning in the dramatic situations
and language of the Petrarchan tradition. Sidney stands close
to the end of that tradition. It is only natural that we should
be able to mark in his work differences of sensibility that
grew out of the time and place in which he wrote. Then
there are the subtler differences that, in any exercise of the
"individual talent," transform and criticize, implicitly or
explicitly, the material with which the poet works.

These remarks are by way of prologue to some more
specific observations about *Astrophel and Stella*. Whatever
familiar figures and dramatic situations Sidney's sonnets

employ, they devote less attention to the continuing and brilliant presentations of the poet's mistress than Petrarch gives to his visions of Laura. It is not that Sidney has drastically altered the roles of lover and lady. The mistress keeps her unattainable state, a fixed star; but there is less wonder in the poet's response, and his admiration has less power to reconcile him to his suffering. A reading of *Astrophel and Stella* must take into consideration this observable shift in the poet's attention; Stella's position is often taken for granted, and a great deal of poetic vitality is absorbed in Astrophel's impatience, in his energetic attempt to disentangle what is and what is not satisfactory in Petrarchan love.

In one of Sidney's best sonnets (number 71), we have a rare example of what appears to be a direct response to a poem by Petrarch.[13] Juxtaposing the sonnets will provide some indication of the direction Sidney takes:

> Chi vuol veder quantunque pò Natura
>   e'l Ciel tra noi, venga a mirar costei,
>   ch'è sola un sol, non pur a li occhi mei,
>   ma al mondo cieco, che vertù non cura;
> e venga tosto, perché Morte fura
>   prima i migliori, e lascia star i rei;
>   questa, aspettata al regno delli dei,
>   cosa bella mortal, passa, e non dura.
> Vedrà, s'arriva a tempo, ogni vertute,
>   ogni bellezza, ogni real costume,
>   giunti in un corpo con mirabil tempre:
> allor dirà che mie rime son mute,
>   l'ingegno offeso dal soverchio lume:
>   ma se più tarda, avrà da pianger sempre.*

(Rime, 248)

*Whoever wishes to see what Nature and Heaven can do among us, come to gaze at her, who alone is a sun, not only to my eyes, but to the blind world which does not care for virtue. And let him come soon, because Death steals away the best first, and leaves the bad behind. She, awaited in the

Who will in fairest booke of Nature know,
  How Vertue may best lodg'd in beautie be,
  Let him but learne of *Love* to reade in thee,
  Stella, those faire lines, which true goodnesse show.
There shall he find all vices' overthrow,
  Not by rude force, but sweetest soveraigntie
  Of reason, from whose light those night-birds flie;
  That inward sunne in thine eyes shineth so.
And not content to be Perfection's heire
  Thy selfe, doest strive all minds that way to move,
  Who marke in thee what is in thee most faire.
So while thy beautie drawes the heart to love,
  As fast thy Vertue bends that love to good:
  'But ah,' Desire still cries, 'give me some food.'

                         (*AS,* 71)

These sonnets, each a fine and characteristic achievement, reflect profound differences in attitude. Petrarch's poem belongs, in his sequence, among those meant to prepare the reader for Laura's death. It has the poetic qualities we have noted before, exaggerated by the presence and pressure of mortality. The first quatrain claims immense significance for Laura: she is the chief handiwork of Nature and Heaven together; she alone is a sun, illuminating not only the poet's life, but also a blind world that does not care for virtue. Petrarch uses his majestic public manner, opening with hyperbolic praise and a resonant invitation ("chi vuol veder . . .") to join him in admiring this rarity of nature. That compliment is intensified by the next quatrain, which urges us to hurry; death steals away the best first. The effect of the lines is simultaneously to heighten the tone of wonder

---

kingdom of the gods, a beautiful mortal thing, passes and does not remain. He will see, if he arrives in time, every virtue, every beauty, every regal quality, joined in one body with admirable temper. Then he will say that my verses are mute, my talent overwhelmed by excess of light. But if he delays too long, he will have to weep forever.

by emphasizing Laura's fleeting brilliance and to reinforce the note of philosophical gravity ("cosa bella mortal, passa, e non dura") struck earlier by "mondo cieco, che vertù non cura." Tempered by time, desire has disappeared, and the poem gives less sense of Laura's physical presence than sonnet 90 ("Erano i capei") does. Rather, in the sestet, Petrarch stresses general characteristics: a harmony of virtue, beauty, and regal bearing. The poem makes no explicit philosophical statements, but it does, by placing Laura against the background of death and time, make clear the role of the visions of Laura in the sequence. She embodies the refining power of earthly beauty; one suffers if one has not seen her. This sonnet dramatizes in its tone of dazzled admiration the kind of life-giving effect she has upon the poet and upon a world faced with the prospect of her absence.

Sidney's sonnet opens with a promise of the same majestic harmony and ends with a devastating comment on the whole Petrarchan vision. It is a troubled poem, inviting multiple interpretations. For the first thirteen lines Sidney's poem appears to be a version of Petrarch's praise of Laura; then in the last line the poem departs completely from its model and our attention is pivoted to Astrophel, forcing a re-evaluation of all the lines that have come before. Two different views of love are balanced against one another: one, noble and assured; the other, impetuous and unanswerable. It is a curious kind of balancing and testing, thirteen lines against one; but the point of the poem is to show the power of desire to bring a carefully created structure toppling to the ground. There is no danger here that the mistress will die, that the vision will disappear (the cause of anguish in the last line of Petrarch's poem). Astrophel, no matter how much he is exposed to Stella's purifying power, still suffers from unsatisfied desire.

The first thirteen lines of Sidney's sonnet are public praise, impressive and formal, an account of the conventionally accepted power of beauty; the tension of the sonnet depends upon the speaker's involvement, his willing response to beauty's refining power. Sidney echoes Petrarch's opening proclamation: "Who will in fairest booke of Nature know." For the most part, the language of the poem is more abstract than Petrarch's, more explicitly "Platonized." The meaning of "booke of Nature" is not substantially different from that of "quantunque pò Natura / e'l Ciel tra noi," but Sidney's poem develops the metaphor of the book and concerns itself, almost systematically, with the process of learning from Stella. The observer will "know," will "read." Petrarch asks us to see and admire; and he gives us more of a sense of Laura as a woman who *embodies* virtue ("ogni real costume, / giunti in un corpo con mirabil tempre"). A sense of illumination is implicit in the tone and dramatic situation, but is not conveyed as explicitly as it is in Sidney's sonnet. Reason appears on the surface of the latter poem; the symbolic identification of the sun with the inward light of reason is drawn for us.

Sidney disposes his materials to emphasize an almost formalized ladder of virtue, the self-conscious lover initially feeling the way Neoplatonic doctrine says he should feel. He learns to read in Stella "those faire lines, which true goodnesse show." It is a vision made concrete mainly by the direct address to Stella, using her name, and by the delicacy of diction in "sweetest soveraigntie," the effect of which is transmitted by a skillful enjambment to the otherwise colorless "reason" of line 7. The octet gains life most strikingly from the one foreign element, its most concrete detail, the disturbing night-birds. These are presumably vices, whose flight from the light shining in Stella's eyes serves to particularize the power of reason that, up to this point, has been presented abstractly.

The sonnet, with a linking "and," moves into the sestet, which is designed to continue in long smooth clauses the description of Stella's effect upon onlookers. The whole sonnet is pitched toward a climax of activity: "So while thy beautie drawes the heart to love, / As fast thy Vertue bends that love to good." After these lines, which gather up the movement of the entire poem, the sonnet shifts from Astrophel's experiencing the public evaluation of beauty and virtue to a private reaction: " 'But ah,' Desire still cries, 'give me some food.' " It is a telling thrust, defeating all expectation of a harmonious ending for the sonnet and a smooth close to the final couplet. "Still" carries its Elizabethan force of "always" and accents the urgency of Desire's crude and direct imperative; the rhetorical control and promise of lines 12 and 13 ("while . . . beautie drawes . . . heart to love, / As fast . . . Vertue bends . . . love to good") is dissipated by the contrast.

The feelings asserted by the line are of necessity complicated. Astrophel seems to regret his position. In Petrarch's sonnet the poet and the public join in admiring Laura from a distance; Astrophel has been set apart, unable to join the community of those "who marke in thee what is in thee most faire." His position parallels that of the night-birds, forced to fly from the light of reason. The shift of attention from the mistress' perfection to the lover's imperfection is an important one; if it stresses his guilt, it also stresses his vitality. In Astrophel's praise of Stella, we detect a note of strain, particularly in a second reading when we are conscious of the ending to come. He describes his mistress' power more abstractly than Petrarch does, treating love as doctrine to be learned and emphasizing less its grounding

in feeling. The phrase of regret, " 'But ah,' Desire still cries,"
also expresses release from the effort implied in "striving"
to move all minds toward perfection and in "as fast" bend-
ing love to good. Astrophel's is the kind of human response,
stressed by the bluntness of his speech, that is felt by Signora
Emilia after Pietro Bembo's rapt discourse on Platonic love
at the end of *The Courtier.* She "tooke him by the plaite of
hys garment and pluckinge him a little, said: 'Take heede,
Master Peter, that these thoughtes make not your soule also
to forsake the bodye.' " [14]

Astrophel cannot resolve the opposing perceptions of the
sonnet, though he gives full value both to the claims of ideal
beauty and to the energetic promptings of desire. In Sidney's
sequence the burden of interest falls upon unreconciled
conflict in a way that it does not in the more harmonious
sonnets of Petrarch. By presenting love against an extended
backdrop of time, Petrarch can convince us of its refining
power and its stimulus to the imagination; he can make
evaluations that convey some air of order and certainty.
Sidney's sonnets noticeably lack a sense of time and the
bearing of time upon love, a characteristic that distinguishes
them from the sonnets of Shakespeare and other Elizabe-
thans. He chooses to ride on the dial's point of the moment
and to dramatize the demands of appetite on the world of
the ideal. When we think of Sidney as writing in the Petrarchan tradition, then, we should allow for his special version.
His mind is well tuned to the conventional responses to
love, of course; they have shaped his expectations and he
feels them fully enough to find drama in the defeat of expectation. As in the *Arcadia,* the relation of lofty aims to
the immediately destructive nature of love is a subject to
engage the imagination.

The sonnet as Sidney uses it in *Astrophel and Stella* proves
to be a form supple enough for his drama. He has moved

away from the static repetitions and parallel structure that lend strength to the laments in the *Arcadia*. He has also abandoned the open rhyme scheme of Surrey for a version of the tighter Italian sonnet. The most common form used in *Astrophel and Stella* is ABBA/ABBA/CDC/DEE.[15] Sidney retains the final couplet of the Surrey scheme, but seldom uses it for purposes of witty summary as he did in the *Arcadia*. In fact, the formalities of the rhyme scheme conceal rather than reveal the movement of a sonnet like "Who will in fairest booke of Nature know." Sidney fills out his sonnets completely and very often works from a generally held view of love to the private reaction of Astrophel, which he reserves as a surprising or qualifying comment in the last line. The sonnet in these cases builds toward a climax in line 13 and defeats our expectations in form as well as content by using the last line of the couplet as contrast, not to complete an epigram. The subtle movement of the sestet of sonnet 71 should illustrate the point. Three kinds of articulation are at work there. The organization by rhyme, CDCD/EE, is countered by the grammatical arrangement; the six lines fall into three sentences CDC/DE/E. The linking rhyme "love" (D) mutes the first grammatical separation and continues the important movement of meaning that divides the first five lines of the sestet from line 14, the urgent " 'But ah,' Desire still cries, 'give me some food.' " This last articulation, CDCDE/E, is the one that the reader notices first, but his experience of the sestet is richer because of the interlocking of divisions by grammar and by rhyme. For none of the usual or expected separations — a sentence ending or a completed rhyme — is allowed to stop us in our reading; this reinforces the effect of "strive" and "drawes." But where one expects continuity — a completion of the final couplet — just there the guillotine falls.

Sidney's main adaptation or innovation in the sonnet form

lies in his handling of the sestet. He seems to prefer the Petrarchan octet; with its two rhymes (in contrast to Surrey's four) and its closed pattern (ABBA/ABBA rather than ABAB/CDCD), it buttresses the single well-knit statement. Sonnet 71 is an excellent example of such harmonies. For the sestet, and particularly for the last line of the poem, he reserves the ironic comment, the sudden agile criticism of harmonies that have been weighed and appreciated before.

3

The comparison of "Who will in fairest booke of Nature know" with its Petrarchan model takes us now to the center of poetic interest in *Astrophel and Stella*. Astrophel can entertain only momentarily the Petrarchan vision of earthly beauty that restores the lover to grace or wisdom. His significant activity is the discovery of conflict, and he delights in it. Astrophel moves freely back and forth between poles marked, on the one hand, by the conventionally defined roles of lover and lady and, on the other, by the attitude expressed with more certainty at a later time by Donne: "Love's not so pure, and abstract, as they use / To say, which have no Mistresse but their Muse." He participates in and then questions traditional attitudes. As in sonnet 71, Astrophel's role in this sequence is that of critic — he tests conventions without necessarily transforming them.

Sidney announces his restiveness and his questioning of conventional attitudes toward love at the very opening of *Astrophel and Stella*. Sonnet 1 is well known:

> Loving in truth, and faine in verse my love to show,
>   That the deare She might take some pleasure of my paine:
>   Pleasure might cause her reade, reading might make her know,
>   Knowledge might pitie winne, and pitie grace obtaine,

I sought fit words to paint the blackest face of woe,
  Studying inventions fine, her wits to entertaine:
  Oft turning others' leaves, to see if thence would flow
  Some fresh and fruitfull showers upon my sunne-burn'd braine.
But words came halting forth, wanting Invention's stay,
  Invention, Nature's child, fled step-dame Studie's blowes,
  And others' feete still seem'd but strangers in my way.
Thus great with childe to speake, and helplesse in my throwes,
  Biting my trewand pen, beating my selfe for spite,
  'Foole,' said my Muse to me, 'looke in thy heart and write.'

(*AS*, 1)

The sonnet opens *Astrophel and Stella* with a fanfare justifying Nashe's exuberant preface to the 1591 edition. It is
a sonnet about style, the relation of style to matter, and it
makes its declaration in splendid, controlled alexandrines,
drawing the reader's attention immediately to the boldness
of the sequence and to its capacity, at will, to vary from the
accepted pentameter line. Most of the poems in fact utilize
a five-foot line, and most of them follow a common rhyme
scheme. But it is not until sonnet 7 that Sidney first repeats
a form exactly, as if to remind us through the variety of the
first sonnets of a latent versatility, a sleeping strength, in
what we are to read. Such maneuvers are playful and self-
conscious, characteristic of *Astrophel and Stella*. For Sidney's sequence asks wakefulness of its readers and raises
doubts that, as sonnet 71 illustrates, it does not always attempt to resolve.

What kind of alertness do the poems demand? As Rosemond Tuve has pointed out, the surprises are not those a
modern reader might expect. The last line of sonnet 1 does
not register a broad claim for "the natural feeling of the
heart, rebelliously bursting through the trammels of form.
Sidney says 'look in thy heart and write,' but he is talking
about 'inventing' or finding matter." [16] The complaint is not

against art, but against false art. The poet is asked to devise, to find conceits that make fully articulate the strength and particularity of his love: in Gascoigne's words, "what Theame soever you do take in hande, if you do handle it but *tamquam in oratione perpetua,* and never studie for some depth of devise in the Invention, and some figures also in the handlyng thereof, it will appeare to the skilfull Reader but a tale of a tubbe." [17] The occasions for invention, he goes on to say, are infinite; there are no firm rules, but the poet can at least begin by avoiding the trite and the obvious: "If I should undertake to wryte in prayse of a gentlewoman, I would neither praise hir christal eye, nor hir cherrie lippe, etc."

To be told then, as Astrophel is told at the end of sonnet 1, to look into one's heart and write is to be reminded of the *source* of eloquence in love poetry. There are several traditions that account for what Astrophel finds when he "looks." For one thing, the heart is the traditional dwelling place of Cupid or Love.[18] But a more relevant strength of the heart in Renaissance poetry is that it holds the image of the poet's mistress. Sidney accepts this as a commonplace in a later sonnet:

> Whence hast thou Ivorie, Rubies, pearle and gold,
> To shew her skin, lips, teeth and head so well?
> 'Foole," answers he, 'no *Indes* such treasures hold,
> But from thy heart, while my sire charmeth thee,
> Sweet *Stella's* image I do steale to mee.'
>
> (*AS,* 32)

"Looke in thy heart and write" may be read as a call to order, pointing out to Astrophel that Stella's image is the source of his powers of invention. The substance of the line is entirely conventional. But the manner of its presentation is not: the violence and release of tension with which the poet is advised to look at Stella's image marks Sidney's version as quite special. He presents this conclusion as a personal discovery, marking it with a burst of direct speech and colloquial reproof ("Foole") that hardly befits the dignity of the supposed Muse who warns him.

In its manner the poem both shares in and calls into question a *merely* public courtly mode. Astrophel opens with a recognition that "loving in truth" requires with it participation in a world of courtly gesture, "her wits to entertaine." If any tension exists between the poet and that world, it is certainly not evident in the elegant balance and rhetorical polish of the opening lines. The octet consists of one sentence whose subject, "I," does not appear until line 5 and whose movement is sustained by strongly accented participles ("loving," "studying," "turning") and the elaborate rhetorical flourish of the opening ("pleasure . . . / Pleasure . . . reade, reading . . . know, / Knowledge . . . pitie . . . pitie grace").[19] The smoothness and facility of these lines help to characterize the world of "inventions fine" and the civilized pleasures of expressive love poetry.

Yet the activity of the octet seems to be in vain. Quite systematically, the sestet denies the efforts of lines 5–8 and sets out Astrophel's frustrations in lines 9–11: the "fit words" he seeks "came halting forth"; in "Studying inventions fine," he succeeds in frightening Invention away; and "turning others' leaves" he finds them "strangers in my way."[20] A study of courtly verse, instead of helping him, accounts for his "sunne-burn'd braine." This striking phrase refers to an accepted Elizabethan figure for poetic imitation. Thomas Wilson, recommending imitation of the ancients, used it in a simile: "For if they that walke much in the Sunne and thinke not of it, are yet for the most part Sunne burnt, it can not be but that they which wittingly and willingly travayle to counterfect each other, must needes take some colour of them." [21] But where Wilson and other rhetoricians urge imitation, Sidney distrusts its ease and sees some danger in it. He draws out what is implicit in the metaphor, the parched sense of the man who has walked too long in the sun of the ancients.

The poem also plays quite deliberately with the word "invention," which contains in Renaissance rhetoric and poetic theory an implicit complication of meaning.[22] It must be both a "stay" and "Nature's child"; it must provide formal excellence and be fully eloquent in representing the feelings from which the poem springs. In sonnet 1 Astrophel first refers to the "inventions fine" of others, poems that define the convention in which he is trying to write. Then it becomes the "stay," the prop that he gropes for as a support or buttress for his own poetic ideas. By an extension of meaning, it becomes the elusive child of Nature, fleeing "step-dame Studie's blowes." Here it gains animation, a homeliness and vitality of its own, to which the fine inventions are hostile. The growing vividness in characterizing invention is part of the movement of the poem away from "studying" conventional sonnets (with the punning "And others' feete still seem'd but strangers in my way") toward the activity hoped for, the "fresh and fruitfull showers" of line 8. In the final tercet, Sidney prepares a climax remarkably like that of sonnet 71: two lines of summary that bring the poem to a point are followed by a surprising completion in the final couplet. Here (lines 12 and 13) the sharply accented lines each fall into two sections of equal length; the tension of "great with childe" and "helplesse in my throwes" is reinforced and heightened by the alliterative participles, "Biting my trewand pen, beating my selfe for spite." All the frustrations of the poem are finally dispelled by the energetic outburst associated with the discovery of Stella's image in the heart. The effect of the poem depends upon contrasting the tightly controlled rhetorical pattern of the first thirteen lines with the monosyllabic directness, the imperatives, the surprising colloquialism, of the last line (which breaks into the poem with only a tenuous syntactical connection to what precedes it).

The interesting point about this sonnet is the self-conscious necessity that Sidney feels to act out, here at the very beginning of the sequence, the process of true invention and to portray it in part as youthful (a victim of step-dame Study), plain-talking, and explosive. But it is equally interesting that the sonnet does not disclaim artifice and convention. With its elaborate rhetorical figures and its attention to Stella's image, it uses a formal literary manner and sonnet conventions quite ostentatiously. Still, it proceeds toward an ironic reminder of the energy that lies behind artifice, and it associates the conventionally hallowed image of the mistress with that reminder.

Astrophel is hostile throughout the sequence toward those who seem to be indulging a merely literary fancy.[23] This distrust makes itself felt in the numerous poems about style, whose presence in *Astrophel and Stella* is one of the marks distinguishing it from other Elizabethan sequences. These poems continue the gesture of the opening sonnet, the professions of independence from courtly wits, and they specify some of the affectations of contemporary love poetry: in sonnet 6, the Petrarchan oxymorons ("living deaths, deare wounds, faire stormes, and freesing fires"), mythological poems, pastoral tales; in sonnet 15, excessive alliteration and "poore Petrarch's long deceased woes"; in sonnet 28, "allegorie's curious frame." Like sonnet 1, though without its comic energy, each of these sonnets returns to Stella, in order to stress the particularity and directness of the poet's love for her: "*Stella* behold, and then begin to endite" (sonnet 15); or "I in pure simplicitie, / Breathe out the flames which burne within my heart, / *Love* onely reading unto me this arte" (sonnet 28).

Critics have been disturbed by the seeming contradiction between the speaker's professions of simplicity and the poems that use the very modes Astrophel distrusts.[24] Sidney does use mythology (five of the first fifteen poems are fables involving Cupid), and he frequently invokes the Petrarchan contraries. We are bound to be puzzled if we take Astrophel's poems on style as a program of reform rather than as a series of rather troubled and self-conscious gestures. His straining after sincerity suggests an uncertainty about the inherited vocabulary of love poetry. His sonnets, at some points, attempt to recover the energy in that tradition and, at other points, to chafe at its limitations and the distorted uses to which it had been put.

4

I began these preliminary remarks on *Astrophel and Stella* by saying that the sequence noticeably lacked the sustained and sustaining visions of the poet's lady that made Petrarch's cycle one of meditation on earthly beauty and its continuing effect on the imagination. Without dethroning Stella, Sidney's sonnets shift a great deal of the energy and poetic attention to Astrophel. The two major sonnets we have been considering, 1 and 71, suggest that inherited attitudes cannot fully express Astrophel's feelings. The dialogue form in which both poems are cast (with line 14 countering the rest of the sonnet) is for that reason important to Sidney; in the final line of both sonnets he presses Astrophel's claims of singularity against an accepted public manner. Once we have understood the demands of desire upon virtue in a sonnet like 71, we are in an even better position to appreciate in sonnet 1 the mocking discomfort of Astrophel in the presence of conventional courtly poetry. Conflict, as expressed in the two poems, exists at different levels of intensity. Sonnet 1 springs from a satirical impulse directed against affectations in literary manner, against love poetry as a court game, concealing the emotions it was intended to convey. The poet appeals to Invention, as he later appeals to the "booke of Nature" written in Stella's features. Sonnet 71 shows, further, how complicated the book of Nature can be for him, when the wonder and dignity of Stella come into abrupt conflict with the urgencies of desire. Renaissance love poetry, of course, thrives on conflict. What sets Sidney's apart is the continued pointing of the poems toward the *discovery* of conflict, the frequent emphasis on disruption itself.

Astrophel's definition of "loving in truth" is a complicated matter, as one might gather from his claims to particularity. As Hallett Smith puts it: "He constantly mentions the difference between himself and others. Distinctiveness, not variety of feeling, is thus important." [25] There is more variety than Smith suggests — we have already noted the shift in feeling between sonnet 1 and sonnet 71, between the satirical criticism of affectation and a poem that passionately specifies the dilemma of the critic. These are poems of definition. We do not depend upon the certain grounds for love that provide the base of Petrarch's sonnets, but upon the sonnet-by-sonnet distinctions made by Astrophel. Astrophel's role is one of sustained alertness and questioning in exercises of a varied sensibility. We never are allowed to rest with an attitude, a gesture; for the next sonnet may exactly contradict an expressed view or remind us that a particular experience is momentary or that a newly discovered truth leads only to further complexities. Our delight depends more firmly upon the persona the poet creates for us — that of the questioning critic — than it does in the more impersonal sonnets of Petrarch. A closer look at Astrophel's progress through the Sidney sequence should bear this out.

5

THE SEQUENCE

THE TERM "sonnet sequence" is as bedeviling as the designation "novel" and tells us even less about the content of a literary work. Renaissance sonneteers did not know their collections as "sequences," and the word must apply to the very different achievements of Sidney, Shakespeare, and Spenser. So, rather than giving a clue to a poet's intention, "sonnet sequence" depends for its definition upon the practice of individual poets, upon the advantages poets may find in setting sonnets in tandem. *Astrophel and Stella* comes closer than most groups of sonnets to telling a story. But the plot is a familiar one, "the tragicomedy of love . . . the argument cruel chastity, the prologue hope, the epilogue despair."[1] Chaucer's *Troilus* must indeed have been, as Gabriel Harvey put it,[2] one of "Astrophel's cordialls," though Astrophel has even less success with his lady. Yet the familiarity of plot, the poet's assumption that his audience has read many narratives of courtly pursuit, is a liberating one. It allows him to focus on the drama of Astrophel's awareness. In the discrete units of a series of sonnets, Astrophel acts out this role of critic and lover, adopting different poses and attitudes toward the conventions of Petrarchan love. We must look for shifts of viewpoint rather than for narrative progression.

1

Astrophel warns us from the outset that it is not only in sonnets about poetry that he exercises his critical function. He begins immediately in sonnet 2 to fulfill the claims to particularity of the opening poem of the sequence:

> Not at first sight, nor with a dribbed shot
>> *Love* gave the wound, which while I breathe will bleed:
>> But knowne worth did in mine of time proceed,
>> Till by degrees it had full conquest got.
> I saw and liked, I liked but loved not,
>> I loved, but straight did not what *Love* decreed:
>> At length to *Love's* decrees, I forc'd, agreed,
>> Yet with repining at so partiall lot.
> Now even that footstep of lost libertie
>> Is gone, and now like slave-borne *Muscovite,*
>> I call it praise to suffer Tyrannie;
> And now employ the remnant of my wit,
>> To make my selfe beleeve, that all is well,
>> While with a feeling skill I paint my hell.
>
> (*AS,* 2)

Astrophel does not love at first sight as true Petrarchans do, nor does the mood set by the poem suggest Petrarch's consuming vision renewed constantly in the mind. The controlled chain of words that represents the action of falling in love ("I saw and liked, I liked but loved not, / I loved . . .") lends dignity to love ("knowne worth did in mine of time proceed") and pays tribute to its inevitability once Astrophel has seen Stella. But it is also a concession, evaluated soberly and ironically as a "partiall lot." Behind the poem lies a world of competing values that Astrophel respects and wistfully looks back to — a world recalled by "lost libertie" and "remnant of my wit." The particular success of this sonnet lies in Sidney's capacity to suggest two aspects of Astrophel's experience: the intensity of his love and, at the same time, regret for the world left behind with its stability, its poise embodied in the controlled tone of the early lines of the poem. By line 14, the staccato manner of describing his experience ("I saw and liked, I liked but loved not, I loved . . .") has given way to more intense expression ("While with a feeling skill I paint my hell"). But this suffering at the end includes more than the complaint of an unrequited lover because it gathers in as well the backward glance at Astrophel's old world, his consciousness of lost freedom and civilized balance.

Using military metaphors to describe love's conquest is common in erotic poetry, a way of representing the elegant maneuvers of Cupid against the lover. But here military terms contribute to the creation of a persona. They serve to characterize Astrophel as plain-speaking: with soldierly directness he admits that Cupid's is not a "dribbed shot" and grudgingly recognizes conquest and enemy "decrees." Such details — along with the colloquial terseness of "slave-borne *Muscovite*" — contribute to the tone of masculine reasonableness that marks Sidney's sonnets off from others. As Lamb noted, these poems bring into love poetry "action, pursuits, studies, feats of arms, the opinion of contemporaries, and his [Astrophel's] judgment of them." [3] But the full importance of such concreteness is to remind us of the heroic education of Astrophel and of the milieu he must leave behind. He first describes his love for Stella in terms of the properties — including the opinions and beliefs — of his own world. Sidney begins, as he did in the *Arcadia*, with active, public life, "full, material, and circumstantiated." [4] These are the poetic counters used in the opening evaluation of love. After sonnet 21, it is always Stella who is his "wit" and his "virtue" but, to begin, he pays at least ironic tribute to another world of wit and virtue that values his love as "will," contrary to "reason." He speaks of his "young mind marde" and complains

> That *Plato* I read for nought, but if he tame
> Such coltish gyres, that to my birth I owe
> Nobler desires, least else that friendly foe,
> Great expectation, weare a traine of shame.
>
> (*AS*, 21)

The world in which he has been trained, and which he abandons, fosters austere notions of public responsibility and a hostility to love. These values, weighed in the early poems, provide an alternative framework for judgment. They help to define Astrophel's sensibility and account for his uncertain acceptance of Petrarchan love; they serve as a springboard for his critical forays. The early sonnets prepare us for his willingness to see love as destructive and for the conflicts of a sonnet like 71: " 'But ah,' Desire still cries, 'give me some food.' "

Though Astrophel's sober heroic studies may sound like unpromising material for love poetry, the fall away from the grace of heroic reason is a rich source of poetic vitality. Sonnet 5 presents the world of reason and the world of love in delicate balance:

> It is most true, that eyes are form'd to serve
> The inward light: and that the heavenly part
> Ought to be king, from whose rules who do swerve,
> Rebels to Nature, strive for their owne smart.
> It is most true, what we call *Cupid's* dart,
> An image is, which for our selves we carve;
> And, fooles, adore in temple of our hart,
> Till that good God make Church and Churchman starve.
> True, that true Beautie Vertue is indeed,
> Whereof this Beautie can be but a shade,
> Which elements with mortall mixture breed:

> True, that on earth we are but pilgrims made,
> And should in soule up to our countrey move:
> True, and yet true that I must *Stella* love.

The poetic material is little more than a series of moral axioms. Its metaphors are not striking: reason as the "inward light," "the heavenly part," king of a man's actions; worship of Cupid as idolatry. Indeed the poem depends, as most of Sidney's sonnets do, on skillful dramatic organization, on his sense of the sonnet as a form to be filled out strategically. In sonnet 5 he speaks as if replying to one of the logic-loving moralists of the public world. As he repeats "It is most true," he conveys ironic reservation in the tone of a lesson learned perhaps too well. Yet there is also respect for the gravity of the moral world, for an order where things are "form'd to serve." And there is appreciation of the possible release for pilgrims who "in soule up to our countrey move."

The poem relies for its success on the accelerated repetition of "true" (twice in the octet, five times in the sestet) and on the response in the reader's mind as Sidney toys with the word's meaning. (He produces wry, playful discomfort in a line that insists as much on truth as line 9 does: "True, that true Beautie Vertue is indeed.") He reaps his harvest in the last line, gathering all the rhetorical force of the poem behind its contrary "true"s: the truth of the rest of the poem and the truth that he must love Stella. The closing phrase strikes the first personal note in the poem and gains all its effect from the contrasting immediacy. The simple assertion of the final line balances the precepts of the preceding thirteen. As Stella's lover, Astrophel is willing to place himself among the "rebels to Nature." He agrees to be considered a fool of love and to accept the private guilt of a worshiper of Cupid who carves his own image of Cupid's dart. He does not, in other words, upset the argument of the poem by denying it. But, conscious of it, in the imperative "must" and the brevity of statement, he asserts impatience and a present urgency that exist on a completely different level from the timeless definitions of the rest of the poem. He confounds his opponents by constructing what appears to be a logical argument ending in paradox. But, in the tone of the reasonable man, he neatly questions the sobriety of such logic with a straightforward reminder that "truth" involves not only what should be but what is.

The sonnet does not, when read, sound as stern as analysis makes it out to be. The argument fleshed out moves toward a graceful compliment to Stella; as soon as the possibility is admitted that her beauty is a "shade" of true beauty, the diction begins to soften and the impatience with abstract argument to reach its height. A great deal of critical praise has been devoted to Sidney's colloquialism and plain speech. We find in this poem, as we did in sonnets 1 and 71, that the directness of speech comes as a dramatic response to a more formal structure and depends for its effect upon it. The noticeable release of tension ("True, and yet true that I must *Stella* love") is also, as it is in other sonnets that use this technique, a recognition of conflict. In sonnet 71, desire shatters the vision of Stella; at this early stage, in sonnet 5, conflict lies in the breaking of philosophic harmony when Astrophel falls in love. But in both cases the plain speech of Astrophel is poised against more abstract assertions and patterned language. Astrophel values philosophical harmony, but finds his delight and energy in the humanizing love that disrupts it. The two points of view are never reconciled.

To evaluate earthly beauty against a philosophical background is a frequent concern of Renaissance love poems. But Sidney's manner is arresting; here again, in sonnet 5, he pitches his verses toward the *discovery* of tensions and discord. Shakespeare handles a related theme very differently (sonnet 60):

> Time doth transfix the flourish set on youth
> And delves the parallels in beauty's brow,
> Feeds on the rarities of nature's truth,
> And nothing stands but for his scythe to mow.

Despite the overwhelming consciousness of mortality in these lines, Shakespeare transmits a sense of sequence and dignity to the process of change. Equal value is given to beauty ("the flourish set on youth") and to the perception that it has what Sidney calls "mortall mixture." The reader is made to feel that there is a medium of judgment working in each line, which gives due weight to contraries, to time's "feeding" and the "rarities of nature's truth." Because of the mature voice of his sonnets, Shakespeare's lines mute — but do not blur — the inescapable conflicts, and they knit together the worlds of process and permanence so that these do not seem to exist independently of one another. For this reason the complexity of many of the best Shakespeare sonnets is conveyed from the very beginning, and the couplets, as it is so often remarked, carry little poetic weight. Shakespeare's splendid periods (often one sentence, patterned grammatically "When . . . then . . .") signify a philosophical judgment that is sure of the place of individual experience; this poet has had to balance his feelings of love against a continuing consciousness of time and change.

Sidney, by contrast, seldom strikes off a line as complex as those I have quoted from Shakespeare. His phrases lack the compressed power and inclusiveness of Shakespeare's "transfix the flourish set on youth." We have had enough experience now with his brilliant use of the final line in some of his sonnets to see that Sidney expresses his sense of complexity in a different way — by quick reversals that call into question attitudes that have preceded them. Sidney's sonnets seldom evaluate beauty so fully as Shakespeare's do. They pay tribute to it by dramatizing its disruptive power in what Sidney portrays as the immediate sweet discord of love. As sonnet 5 illustrates, Sidney keeps two attitudes toward beauty separate from one another. Astrophel is a speaker committed to the persuasions of the moment; love makes him a critic of philosophical judgment rather than its poetic exponent.

2

Like Pyrocles and Musidorus, Astrophel is at first concerned with his abandonment of heroic reason. "Reason's audite," a phrase from sonnet 18, describes the process of self-examination that occupies much of the first third of the sequence.[5] Astrophel's love for Stella presents a direct challenge to the training and expectations of the active life:

> Your words my friend (right healthfull caustiks) blame
> My young mind marde, whom *Love* doth windlas so,
> That mine owne writings like bad servants show
> My wits, quicke in vaine thoughts, in vertue lame:
> That *Plato* I read for nought, but if he tame
> Such coltish gyres, that to my birth I owe
> Nobler desires, least else that friendly foe,
> Great expectation, weare a traine of shame.
> For since mad March great promise made of me,
> If now the May of my yeares much decline,
> What can be hoped my harvest time will be?
> Sure you say well, your wisdome's golden mine,
> Dig deepe with learning's spade, now tell me this,
> Hath this world ought so faire as *Stella* is?
>
> (*AS*, 21)

Like sonnet 5 ("It is most true"), sonnet 21 defends Astrophel against a call to public responsibility, though here the attacker is a friend and the defense less formal, with its familiar "Sure" and its parenthetical "my friend." In the public view, urged by his friend, love is "coltish" and irrational, a self-inflicted wound; it hunts him down and ensnares him. ("Windlas" in this context refers to a method of capturing game within a circular enclosure.) The speaker gives solemn dignity to the public world by personifying it as "great expectation," and he embodies order in a splendid image of the natural curve of the hero's career: his "mad March," the "May of [his] yeares," the "harvest time." Having characterized love as disorderly, as outside the sequence of nature, the poem moves in its final lines quietly and firmly toward Astrophel's reply, which completely ignores his friend's "right healthfull caustiks." Astrophel's reply has little to do with the rest of the poem; it merely stands beside it, independent of its judgment, a question naively asked and prompted by the claims of the moment against the general claims, the seasons of duty in the rest of the sonnet.

Sonnet 18 employs the same technique, working again from regret ("With what sharpe checkes I in my selfe am shent, / When into Reason's audite I do go") toward a quiet compliment to Stella ("I see and yet no greater sorow take, / Then that I lose no more for *Stella's* sake"). This time the tone is formal and meditative, with Astrophel imagining himself as a prodigal son who counts himself a bankrupt "Of all those goods, which heav'n to me hath lent." Again when he has stated the case for virtue, reason, and wit, and judged that he has "lost himself," he counters the movement of the poem by simply asserting the rights of the private voice that enters with an unaccented break into the thirteenth line. There is no attempt at reconciliation, but rather a shrugging gesture of abandonment. Neither 18 nor 21 presents its case for love with as much release of dramatic tension as sonnet 5 does. They do their work more gently, and cheerfully move away from the claims of philosophy and the world's wisdom.

There are other ways Sidney marks the divorce of love and philosophy in the opening sonnets. At times the claims of reason and virtue are taken less seriously and become irritants. Sonnets 4 and 10 should be read side by side in this connection:

> *Vertue* alas, now let me take some rest,
>   Thou setst a bate betweene my will and wit,
>   If vaine love have my simple soule opprest,
>   Leave what thou likest not, deale not thou with it.
> Thy scepter use in some olde *Catoe's* brest;
>   Churches or schooles are for thy seate more fit:
>   I do confesse, pardon a fault confest,
>   My mouth too tender is for thy hard bit.
> But if that needs thou wilt usurping be,
>   The litle reason that is left in me,
>   And still th'effect of thy perswasions prove:
> I sweare, my heart such one shall shew to thee,
>   That shrines in flesh so true a Deitie,
>   That *Vertue*, thou thy selfe shalt be in love.
>
> (AS, 4)

> Reason, in faith thou art well serv'd, that still
>   Wouldst brabling be with sence and love in me:
>   I rather wisht thee clime the Muses' hill,
>   Or reach the fruite of Nature's choisest tree,
> Or seeke heavn's course, or heavn's inside to see:
>   Why shouldst thou toyle our thornie soile to till?
>   Leave sense, and those which sense's objects be:
>   Deale thou with powers of thoughts, leave love to will.
> But thou wouldst needs fight both with love and sence,
>   With sword of wit, giving wounds of dispraise,
>   Till downe-right blowes did foyle thy cunning fence:

For soone as they strake thee with *Stella's* rayes,
    Reason thou kneel'dst, and offeredst straight to prove
    By reason good, good reason her to love.

                                                    (*AS*, 10)

Astrophel moves in these sonnets among personified virtues with which he is impatient. He assumes his critical role,
picturing old loyalties in a new light. The textbook oppositions of Reason and Love are too artificial; the textbook
definitions of Virtue and Reason are too narrow if they do
not include his feeling for Stella. The poems end in warm
compliment only when Reason and Virtue submit to her.
The plain-speaking voice that closes so many sonnets in the
sequence here controls entire poems. Virtue and Reason,
not the dignified representatives of the public world — like
"great expectation" in sonnet 21 — are addressed as comic
old masters. Astrophel has wearied of Virtue who, in his
sternness ("pardon a fault confest"), seems to allow no
faults; the tone of weary contempt for Reason again implies a kind of uncomfortable familiarity. For any reader of
Renaissance literature, it is a surprise to hear Reason called
a "brabler" who is "well serv'd" in his defeat. It is equally
strange and amusing to learn that Virtue is a "usurper" and
to find both Reason and Virtue the objects of Astrophel's
strenuous imperatives. Instead of the respect for Virtue's
kingship of sonnet 5 ("the heavenly part / Ought to be
king"), Astrophel sends him packing ("Thy scepter use in
some olde *Catoe's* brest"). The effect of the personifications
in these two sonnets is to set the public world at a comic
distance; they reinforce the impression given by the other
sonnets of the irrelevance of public standards to the private
world of love.

These two poems give the reader a chance to characterize
the plain-speaker of Sidney's sonnets more closely. The lover

is energetic and youthful; he is contemptuous of old Catoes, of churches, schools, the Muses' hill, astronomy, powers of thought. He feels constantly embattled: Virtue sets a "bate" (a contention) between his will and wit, and it rides him hard in his coltish years ("My mouth too tender is for thy hard bit"); Reason "brables" (disputes) and keeps him in motion by attacking "with sword of wit, giving wounds of dispraise." Clearly he sees the public world, with its moral and philosophical truths, in this fashion because he views it through the lens of love.

Though there is in the last tercet of each poem a gentleness not present in the earlier lines ("*Vertue*, thou thy selfe shalt be in love"; "By reason good, good reason her to love"), love is known in a manner proper to desire — by its strength. Thus the conventional language of the compliment to Stella in the last tercet of sonnet 4 (she is again the goddess whose image is in his heart) gains its effect less by convincing us of her virtue than by its gesture of tribute to her power. The poetic vitality of these lines comes from the originality of Astrophel's dramatic pose: the threatened conversion ("if that needs thou wilt usurping be, / . . . I sweare") of Virtue to love. In the same way, the "downe-right blowes" of Stella's glance in sonnet 10 bring Reason to his knees. Both gestures attest the mocking energy that marks Astrophel in love. As in sonnet 5, love in itself does not impart to him any philosophical power; it makes him suspicious of philosophers. He fulfills, with a great deal of wit, the role of critic, accepting the admixture of desire in love as a sign of humanity that the sages seem to have lost.

The sonnets discussed so far have paid tribute to love in terms of what it — happily, to Astrophel's mind — disrupts. Among these exasperated defenses against the public world, sonnet 14 stands out as defining the power of love more positively. Here Astrophel begins, as in sonnets 4 and 10, by defending himself against a disapproving friend and "Rubarb words," but moves to something entirely different in the sestet:

> Alas have I not paine enough my friend,
>> Upon whose breast a fiercer Gripe doth tire
>> Then did on him who first stale downe the fire,
>> While *Love* on me doth all his quiver spend,
> But with your Rubarb words yow must contend
>> To grieve me worse, in saying that Desire
>> Doth plunge my wel-form'd soule even in the mire
>> Of sinfull thoughts, which do in ruine end?
> If that be sinne which doth the maners frame,
>> Well staid with truth in word and faith of deed,
>> Readie of wit and fearing nought but shame:
> If that be sinne which in fixt hearts doth breed
>> A loathing of all loose unchastitie,
>> Then Love is sinne, and let me sinfull be.

> > > > > > > > (*AS*, 14)

In the octet the speaker presents one view of love: not only is it a bird of prey (the "fiercer Gripe" or vulture of line 2), but, according to his chiding friend, it is compounded of desire and brings "sinfull thoughts" to his "wel-form'd soule." As Young points out,[6] the poem is built out of the dramatic contrast between the octet, a single outburst with rough diction and "violently enjambed lines," and the sestet, with its balanced tercets ("If that be sinne . . . If that be sinne") and neat phrasing. The sestet poses a new definition of love, attempting in the process to show up the friend's view of sin as rigid and *merely* conventional. This is Astrophel's fullest attempt in the early sonnets at expressing the virtues of love. In sonnet 5 he had countered the public notion of "truth" with a private assertion, "True, and yet true that I must *Stella* love." But the verbal play on "sin" in sonnet 14 con-

stitutes a full-scale definition. The sestet presents his passionate difference from the friend in the publicly acceptable
form of premise and conclusion. The conditional definition,
with its ironic implications, is appropriate for another
reason: it keeps the friend's narrow standards of virtue before us (in the repeated "sin"). The friend sees love only as
desire; in *his* sense it is sin. Sidney sees it as well in terms of
what it might accomplish: enlightenment that, ironically
enough, the caustic friend would appreciate. The figure of
Prometheus introduced into the poem is relevant; for he is
a sinner in stealing the fire from heaven and suffers for it,
and his act, in human terms, proves beneficial and heroic.

The harmonious sestet of sonnet 14 strikes an unusual
note and gives a foretaste of some sonnets that occur later in
the sequence. But of the two views of love presented in this
poem, it is love considered as desire that predominates in
the opening third of the sequence. Astrophel energetically
welcomes that view and his fallen state. He takes delight in
the self-inflicted wounds:

> It is most true, what we call *Cupid's* dart,
> An image is, which for our selves we carve;
> And, fooles, adore in temple of our hart.
>
> (*AS*, 5)

It is worthwhile keeping this valuation in mind as one reads
a second group of sonnets that complement these defenses
against reason; these sonnets present the exploits of Cupid.
As L. C. John points out, they owe a great deal to the Ana-
creontic conception of Cupid as a winged mischievous child,
a version not really popular in England before the publication of *Astrophel and Stella* in 1591.[7] It is easy to see why
the genre might have had special appeal for Sidney. These
poems take a sly delight in the folly of love — they are exer-

cises in wit, which at the same time reinforce the emphasis on the capricious and disruptive side of love. In this group are sonnets 7, 8, 11, 12, 17, 19, 20, and 29. Most of these poems are either conceited narratives or blazons, the general point being that Cupid's power lies in Stella's physical beauty. Cupid is found "playing and shining in each outward part" (sonnet 11). His chief strength lies in Stella's eyes: "his grandame Nature . . . / Of *Stella's* browes made him two better bowes / And in her eyes of arrowes infinit" (sonnet 17). Though Cupid shines in Stella's features, he has nothing to do with her heart; this theme is the basis of several sonnets (11, 12, 29).

> So *Stella's* heart, finding what power *Love* brings,
> To keepe it selfe in life and liberty,
> Doth willing graunt, that in the frontiers he
> Use all to helpe his other conquerings:
> And thus her heart escapes . . .
>
> (*AS*, 29)

Most of these poems end by shifting their attention from Stella to Astrophel and to the wounds of desire, arbitrarily dispensed by Cupid. Sonnet 7, to take one example, asks a riddle: "When Nature made her chiefe worke, *Stella's* eyes, / In colour blacke, why wrapt she beames so bright?" A number of conceits are suggested as answers: for artistic reasons (Stella's black eyes set off her fair skin); to serve as a black veil to hide the dazzling Platonic light; to show Nature's miraculous power in making black seem beautiful. All these responses are offered tentatively, in the form of questions. The only sure response is the final one:

> . . . she [Nature] minding *Love* should be
> Placed ever there, gave him this mourning weed,
> To honor all their deaths, who for her bleed.
>
> (*AS*, 7)

The witty couplet places a sting in the tail of the poem, as we shift to Astrophel's "death." It is an urbane version of a rather tired conceit, the lover's death at a glance from his mistress, and it succeeds partly because of the ironic shift from praise of Stella's eyes to the one certain thing in the poem, their destructive effect on Astrophel. "Honor" in line 14 implies a self-regarding quality in physical beauty, a delight in collecting and commemorating slain lovers, which lends sharpness and energy to the entire sonnet.

The best of the Cupid sonnets, number 20, is worth detailed consideration:

> Flie, fly, my friends, I have my death wound; fly,
>   See there that boy, that murthring boy I say,
>   Who like a theefe, hid in darke bush doth ly,
>   Till bloudie bullet get him wrongfull pray.
> So Tyran he no fitter place could spie,
>   Nor so faire levell in so secret stay,
>   As that sweete blacke which vailes the heav'nly eye:
>   There himselfe with his shot he close doth lay.
> Poore passenger, passe now thereby I did,
>   And staid pleasd with the prospect of the place,
>   While that blacke hue from me the bad guest hid:
> But straight I saw motions of lightning' grace,
>   And then descried the glistring of his dart:
>   But ere I could flie thence, it pierc'd my heart.
>
> (*AS*, 20)

Sidney takes the simple Renaissance physiology of love, the assumption that love is transmitted through the eyes,[8] and its mythological extension, lovers' glances as Cupid's darts, and imagines this material in the form of a hunting scene. The effect is a triumph of Sidney's dramatic technique; the poem conveys an immediate reaction to love. In his opening imperatives Astrophel suggests all that is needed to set the atmosphere of the lover's first sight of his lady: danger and

a sense of sly deceit. The figure of the hunter hunted becomes vivid through his exclamations and his warnings; he
warns, we presume, a party of male friends and is dramatizing the fall from innocent knighthood against this background of courtly sport. Love as an ambush is presented
playfully — this is a welcome betrayal — and we feel Sidney's
control from the very beginning in the comical exaggera-
tions: the repeated "Flie, fly . . . fly / . . . that boy, that
murthring boy." There are sophisticated compliments for
Stella: her eyes are a fit place for a tyrant to hide. The
"motions of lightning' grace" and "glistring of his dart" add
seductive brightness to deceit, so that by the end of the
poem, the ambush, the "piercing" of his heart, is both wel-
comed and feared; the implication of the opening lines, that
this is mock danger, is realized.

In the sly and urbane atmosphere that Astrophel's voice
conveys, "heav'nly eye" (line 7) lacks fresh poetic effect and
seems a typical "abstract counter" of love poetry, having
little to do with the aspect of love being dramatized in this
poem. The fact does remind us, however, of an important
contrast between Sidney's cycle and Petrarch's, which originally gave poetic life to such counters. In Sidney's sequence,
there are two poems — 2 and 20 — that deal with the actual
process of falling in love, with the poet's first vision of his
mistress. Neither deals with the subject in the most characteristic Petrarchan manner, the sudden illumination of love.
Petrarch's "Erano i capei," we saw in the last chapter, contains a superb example of the experience: "Non era l'andar
suo cosa mortal, / ma d'angelica forma." Petrarch's sonnet
ends by mentioning Cupid's arrow ("Piaga per allentar
d'arco non sana"). But that perception of desire is wedded
dramatically to the substance and tone of the rest of the
poem. By contrast, the plot of Sidney's sonnet "Flie, fly, my

friends" has very little to do with a "heav'nly eye." Sonnets 2 and 20 of *Astrophel and Stella*, though they are effective poems about falling in love, both lack the radiance with which Petrarch envisioned this theme.

What picture do we get of love, then, at the outset of *Astrophel and Stella*? Most of the poetic interest lies in the figure of Astrophel in whom love prompts a series of harried defenses. He is attacked, on the one hand, by reason and responsibilities that he has neglected and, on the other, by love and the appeal of the senses. His defenses are often literally acted out: in sonnet 10 he fences against Reason; in sonnet 20 he is ambushed by Cupid. Always the victim, Astrophel appears to be involved in perpetual conflict, perpetual motion. He moves, a witty commentator, among personified virtues and public demands. Like the lover in Petrarch's sonnets, he is separated by his love from the world around him. But he weighs the claims of that world more strongly than the lover in the *Rime* does. Astrophel has a sense of his own "wel-form'd soule" and an exaggerated consciousness of desire. These factors combine to explain why Sidney is not attracted to two important kinds of sonnets: the vision of love and the pastoral retreat. As used by Petrarch those modes, while giving full weight to desire, dramatize the enrichment of the poet-lover's imagination through memory and separation from his mistress.

Sidney is not as certain as Petrarch about the value of love and the risks of *otium*, though he is certain of love's power and shows delight in his fall from virtue. The voice of Astrophel is almost the opposite of Petrarch's: recognizing conflicts where Petrarch enforces harmonies; tentative and critical where Petrarch is sure about the relation of beauty and philosophic meditation. The rueful, quasi-serious, at times mocking voice that Sidney has developed for Astrophel

is the perfect vehicle for registering his doubts about love
while at the same time conveying love's energy. It is a voice
that can move from irony to graceful praise. Even the Cupid
sonnets, the weakest of the opening group, provide examples; in these elaborate narratives Astrophel can wryly
account for love's capriciousness and still end by compli-
menting Stella. The mastery of persona is what makes the
sonnets of *Astrophel and Stella* a more flexible medium for
writing about love than the sonnets of the *Arcadia*.

3

After sonnet 21, heroic virtue is left behind. Astrophel once
recalls his prelapsarian state: sonnet 47 ("What, have I thus
betrayed my libertie?") closes with a marvelous inner dialogue between a voice that feels public responsibility and a
voice that understands the urgencies of eye and heart. In the
best dramatic tradition of the sequence, the poem ends by
undermining formal rhetoric, here represented by the trum-
peting exhortations to Virtue:

> Vertue awake, Beautie but beautie is,
> I may, I must, I can, I will, I do
> Leave following that, which it is gaine to misse.
> Let her go. Soft, but here she comes. Go to,
> Unkind, I love you not: O me, that eye
> Doth make my heart give to my tongue the lie.
>
> (*AS*, 47)

These calls to the active life express momentary regret.
For the rest of the sequence, Astrophel devotes himself to
love, justifying his passion, as the princes did in the *Arcadia*,
by pointing out that love also leads to active goodness. He
is able to declare to Stella (sonnet 64), "Thou art my Wit,
and thou my Vertue art," and thus forcefully identify her
with abstractions that his love for her had originally chal-

lenged, the wit and virtue of the early sonnets. Astrophel's declaration in sonnet 64 comes at the conclusion of a series of violent oaths, which turn his profession into something more than Neoplatonic cliché:

> No more, my deare, no more these counsels trie,
>   O give my passions leave to run their race:
>   Let Fortune lay on me her worst disgrace,
>   Let folke orecharg'd with braine against me crie,
> Let clouds bedimme my face, breake in mine eye,
>   Let me no steps but of lost labour trace,
>   Let all the earth with scorne recount my case,
>   But do not will me from my *Love* to flie.
> I do not envie *Aristotle's* wit,
>   Nor do aspire to *Caesar's* bleeding fame,
>   Nor ought do care, though some above me sit,
> Nor hope, nor wishe another course to frame,
>   But that which once may win thy cruell hart:
>   Thou art my Wit, and thou my Vertue art.

> (*AS*, 64)

The insistence of the poem — its pattern of repeated vows and exclamations — prevents the last line from being merely a Petrarchan formula. Astrophel reminds us of everything that must be given up for Stella: approval of the learned, fame, scholarly wit, achievement, position. The accumulated strength of what has been given up turns the concluding line into forceful declaration.

Astrophel is able in a sonnet like 64 to support with a great deal of energy the leavening belief of good Petrarchans: Stella's earthly beauty as a shadow of the ideal, of virtue and true knowledge. But the power and meaning of Neoplatonic doctrine is something with which he must grapple throughout the latter two thirds of the sequence. His very vitality in sonnet 64 bears the impact of a powerful sensibility that is apt not only to re-create the strengths, but also to chafe at the limitations of Neoplatonic doctrine. Once the reproaches of the active life fade into the distance, there are other challenges to the traditional sovereignty of love. Among these is desire, which appears, as early as sonnet 25, as part of a witty testing of love.

Sonnet 25 leads up to the vision of Stella at the "height of Vertues throne" and brings the Platonists somewhat ironically into support of Astrophel's love for her:

> The wisest scholler of the wight most wise
> > By *Phoebus'* doome, with sugred sentence sayes,
> > That Vertue, if it once met with our eyes,
> > Strange flames of *Love* it in our soules would raise;
> But for that man with paine this truth descries,
> > While he each thing in sense's ballance wayes,
> > And so nor will, nor can, behold those skies
> > Which inward sunne to *Heroicke* minde displaies,
> Vertue of late, with vertuous care to ster
> > Love of her selfe, takes *Stella's* shape, that she
> > To mortall eyes might sweetly shine in her.
> It is most true, for since I her did see,
> > Vertue's great beautie in that face I prove,
> > And find th'effect, for I do burne in love.
>
> (AS, 25)

The sonnet moves playfully down the Platonic ladder. Like sonnet 71, this one goes from the general to the particular. Astrophel places himself quite clearly among those "in sense's ballance" who attempt to apply an abstract lesson to a concrete case ("for I do burne in love"). No one would claim for the sonnet the explicit passionate tension of 71. But this poem similarly weighs the effects of desire against its purer causes, "burning in love" against the "Heroicke minde" and "strange flames." Astrophel begins with appreciative explanation. Presumably he is referring to Plato as "the wisest scholler of the wight most wise" and to the

Phaedrus.⁹ The exegesis is carefully and soberly set out in the octet, but its philosophical vocabulary ("vertue," "sense's ballance," "inward sunne") is shown to be moving toward an elegant praise of Stella, Virtue's model on earth.

Yet there is a certain mockery in Sidney's alliterative presentation ("wisest . . . wight . . . wise / . . . sugred sentence sayes"), in the doubled superlatives ("wisest . . . most wise"), in the idea of philosophy as "sugred sentence," in the hint of Virtue's self-regard ("Vertue of late, with vertuous care to ster / Love of her selfe"). If Astrophel marvels at the descent of Virtue, his account of it is also neatly distant by comparison with the direct feeling of the last line. The final tercet with its deft close sets us off balance, giving us Astrophel's reaction to the fable. Like the ending of 71, it stresses the sting of desire in a simple monosyllabic fragment that punctures the gravity of the rest of the poem. It is a sly conclusion, since we are left to wonder about the effect of Astrophel's desire on its purer parent, the "Strange flames of *Love*" that Virtue would raise in our souls. The ambiguity is maintained, for Astrophel never mentions desire by name; he only suggests it in the double reference of "burne" and in the contrast of Astrophel's urgent plain speech with the scholar's doctrines.

One critic suggests that the "Neoplatonic line of thought promises release from emotional conflicts to Sidney, as also to the far deeper and more impressionable genius of Spenser." ¹⁰ This statement is misleading, first of all, in not distinguishing Sidney from Spenser. In Sidney's case the promise of release is not always realized. Part of the wit of a sonnet like "The wisest scholler of the wight most wise" lies in its implicit suggestion of a gap between Astrophel's experience and the Neoplatonic ideal. He appreciates and expounds that ideal, but savors its complications as well.

There is an informative contrast to be made with Spenser. C. S. Lewis has characterized the *Amoretti* as following a "devout, quiet, harmonious pattern." [11] Lacking the variety of Sidney's sonnets, they also lack (with the notable exception of sonnet 88) the perturbations of desire. Neoplatonic doctrine provides the scaffolding for the following Spenser sonnet as it did for Sidney's sonnet 25:

> Men call you fayre, and you doe credit it,
>> For that your selfe ye dayly such doe see:
>> but the trew fayre, that is the gentle wit,
>> and vertuous mind, is much more praysd of me.
> For all the rest, how ever fayre it be,
>> shall turne to nought and loose that glorious hew:
>> but onely that is permanent and free
>> from frayle corruption, that doth flesh ensew.
> That is true beautie: that doth argue you
>> to be divine and borne of heavenly seed:
>> deriv'd from that fayre Spirit, from whom al true
>> and perfect beauty did at first proceed.
> He onely fayre, and what he fayre hath made,
>> all other fayre like flowres untymely fade.[12]

This poem does not represent Spenser at his best, but it does indicate the order to which his love for his mistress belongs. Spenser's "Epithalamion," printed with the *Amoretti*, best embodies the balance of spirit and sense that marks his version of Neoplatonism. But his sonnet gives us a blueprint, a "type" of the *Amoretti*. It is, to oversimplify, a static sonnet, and it mutes the inherent conflicts with its closely harmonized rhymes (ABAB/BCBC/CDCD/EE). Above all, it keeps the image of Spenser's mistress steadily before us. Sidney, having presented Stella as the "sweetly shining" embodiment of virtue in sonnet 25, shifts away from her to Astrophel's response ("It is most true . . .") in lines that qualify the tribute paid by the rest of the poem to the vir-

tuous mind. Spenser is able to see earthly beauty as a sign
of inner grace in the *Amoretti*. Sidney's reaction is more
complex. For if his sonnets represent attempts by the lover
to value his mistress and to assess the place of her beauty in
the scheme of things, they also remind the reader that beauty
is a temptation.

There are other obstacles besides desire to Astrophel's
full acceptance of the Petrarchan view of love or its Neoplatonic descendants. Sidney's sonnets reveal a sense of the
rapidity with which feeling can turn, in society, into affectation. Astrophel is surrounded by comic figures, grotesques
of the court: "busie wits" (sonnet 30); "dustie wits" (sonnet
26); "curious wits" (sonnet 23). Having escaped the rigorous
masculine standards of the heroic world, he faces another
kind of rigor in the artificialities of the lover's world and
of the "courtly Nymphs" who dominate it:

> Because I breathe not love to everie one,
>   Nor do not use set colours for to weare,
>   Nor nourish speciall lockes of vowed haire,
>   Nor give each speech a full point of a grone,
> The courtly Nymphs, acquainted with the mone
>   Of them, who in their lips *Love's* standerd beare;
>   'What, he?' say they of me, 'now I dare sweare,
>   He cannot love: no, no, let him alone.'
> And thinke so still, so *Stella* know my mind,
>   Professe in deed I do not *Cupid's* art;
>   But you faire maides, at length this true shall find,
>   That his right badge is but worne in the hart:
>   Dumbe Swannes, not chatring Pies, do Lovers prove,
>   They love indeed, who quake to say they love.

> > (*AS*, 54)

To define his own love, Astrophel here gives us a sense
of the way in which courtiers' love and the language of love

poetry have become embalmed, by the sixteenth century, as mere mannerism. The lover's complaint has become "the mone / Of them, who in their lips *Love's* standerd beare"; what was once language adequate to dramatize the lover's state has become a kind of patter designed for a world of elegant promiscuity. This sonnet gives another key to Sidney's dissatisfaction, voiced at the opening of the sequence, with the traditional vocabulary of love, and it helps to explain why so much of the drama of Astrophel's love for Stella should be carried out in poems about style and the definition of words. Astrophel's disdain for "Cupid's art" is not only a product of the critical sensibility revealed in the opening sonnets; it also springs from frustration with a society that has learned its Petrarch too well and has become insensible to the fresh coinage of Petrarchan language. There are moments when Astrophel tries energetically to recreate the Petrarchan spirit. But at other points his recourse is the pose of plain-speaker, the critic and satirist who uses proverbs like that of line 13 above, tendering his confusion and awkwardness rather than his Petrarchan skill as a sign of love.

Astrophel's distrust of the "chatring Pies" of court poetry extends to Stella, who several times in the sequence indulges her literary fancies. Like Orsino in *Twelfth Night*, she has fallen in love with the music of love and becomes the prisoner of it, ignoring Astrophel though attending to his song:

> She heard my plaints, and did not only heare,
>   But them (so sweete is she) most sweetly sing,
>   With that faire breast making woe's darknesse cleare:
> A prety case! . . .   (*AS*, 57)

Sonnet 45 puts his reproach quite clearly:

Stella oft sees the verie face of wo
  Painted in my beclowded stormie face:
  But cannot skill to pitie my disgrace,
  Not though thereof the cause her selfe she know:
Yet hearing late a fable, which did show
  Of Lovers never knowne, a grievous case,
  Pitie thereof gate in her breast such place
  That, from that sea deriv'd, teares' spring did flow.
Alas, if Fancy drawne by imag'd things,
  Though false, yet with free scope more grace doth breed
  Then servant's wracke, where new doubts honor brings;
Then thinke my deare, that you in me do reed
  Of Lover's ruine some sad Tragedie:
  I am not I, pitie the tale of me.

(*AS*, 45)

The sonnet emphasizes the gap that exists between Astrophel as poet and as lover. We may remember how Petrarch balanced these two roles against one another, gaining, for his painful love, enrichment of the imagination. Among the many ironies that arise from the transmission of Petrarchan conventions is the way that they encourage satisfaction with a literary passion and draw attention from the experience on which the original poems were based. In sonnet 45 the separation between poet and mistress is not enforced by a sense of her marvelous presence and dazzling virtue. Stella, in responding to tales rather than to her lover's sorrowful glance, has reduced an imaginative world of love to courtly affectation and literary mannerism. In this poem, Astrophel ironically assents.

Sonnet 45, like sonnet 25, straightforwardly presents the external circumstances that, it becomes apparent to the reader, falsify the lover's feelings. The lover's criticisms in both poems are revealed without a break in the tone of civility that Stella's courtly world imposes. On the surface, sonnet 45 is an elegant narrative, describing Stella's behavior in the octet and imploring her grace in the sestet. While valuing her pity, the poem makes it amply clear how much of his own energy Astrophel must surrender. He begins with a self-possessed public address: in the first quatrain he recounts her scorn of him; in the second, her contrasting pity for the lovers in a fable. However, in the sestet he turns to Stella (abandoning third-person reference to her for direct address) and consents, with a simple "alas," to the absurdities of line 14.

Sonnet 45 provides an ironic answer to the question these sonnets keep examining: the extent to which love leads to active virtue and offers an alternative to the public life Astrophel has been forced to renounce. Accepting Stella's world in this poem, he reduces his declarations of love to barbed and elegant ironies, a parody of the traditional relation of lover and lady. In *Astrophel and Stella* entrance into the world of love does not release Astrophel from his role as critic and open to him its own fields of philosophy. Courtly affectation transforms the rich vocabulary of Petrarchan poetry into a set of jaded maneuvers; the mistress' claims to virtue appear in a self-regarding, prideful light. At other points, desire threatens to break the lover's bond of patience. For all these reasons, the roles of critic and naif — in Astrophel's continual testing — are appropriate and convenient ones by which he can define his love. As the excerpts in this section have emphasized, Astrophel's position in relation to Stella is not constant and established in quite the way that Petrarch's is toward Laura.

It would be misleading, furthermore, to suggest that Astrophel adopts any uniform tone when he performs his critical role. Good-humored mockery is very often his motive rather than the revelation of any deep tension or conflict. He can project himself quite exuberantly into Stella's world:

"Deare, why make you more of a dog then me?" (*AS*, 59)
As Rosemond Tuve points out, this poem is "a string of
suggested possible causes," each rejected because the poet
feels he has the virtue named to a more attractive degree
than Stella's pet has.[13] Astrophel's possession of wit is the
principal difference between them. He can only conclude:

> Alas, if you graunt only such delight
> To witlesse things, then *Love* I hope (since wit
> Becomes a clog) will soone ease me of it.

The whole poem has been a display of wit, one the Renaissance reader would be expected to feel as a logical *tour de
force*. So Astrophel's expectations of losing his wit have a
double-edged charm: a reminder of what he would give
up for affectionate treatment and a reminder that wit is
responsible for the persuasive power of the poem that the
mistress has just enjoyed reading. Sidney is a master of this
kind of humorous praise; it involves him in courtly compliment while keeping him and his lady aware of its absurdities.

4

In the preceding section I have set out some of the elements of Astrophel's experience once he has entered the
world of love: on one hand, the lofty aims of love; on the
other, the disruptive claims of desire and the affectations of
the courtly world. We shall see now, in following the order
of the poems more closely, how the sonnets are compounded
of these forces in varying strengths and, when read in sequence, qualify one another so as to keep the reader in a
state of uncertainty. Petrarch's sonnets considered as a sequence create the impression of concentric rings of experience moving outward from the single epiphany, his vision
of Laura. The progression of Sidney's sequence is linear.

We often find him questioning and redefining his attitudes, rather than reinforcing or deepening an initial impression. This is a new role for the traditionally restless lover, this search for some certain cause of his restlessness. The section that follows begins to trace the arc of that experience in the second quarter of the sequence, trying to discover some patterns in the order in which the sonnets have been given to us.

Richard Young is right in saying that a new movement in *Astrophel and Stella* crystallizes in the sonnets numbered in the low 30s. The preceding sonnets have acted out the withdrawal from the world of heroic reason, thereby "establishing love as the central and single value, with Stella as its symbol." [14] But the poems suggest almost immediately Astrophel's doubts about love. The opening poem of the sequence had asked him to look into his heart, to write from Stella's image. As Young suggests, sonnet 34 is almost a reprise of sonnet 1; in it the poet again faces the task of writing about love. "But the linked clauses that expressed the laborious study in the first sonnet are replaced by a technique of question and answer, expressing a sense of crippled purpose." [15]

> Come let me write, 'And to what end?' To ease
>   A burthned hart. 'How can words ease, which are
>   The glasses of thy dayly vexing care?'
>   Oft cruell fights well pictured forth do please.
>
>   . . . . .
>
> 'What idler thing, then speake and not be hard?'
>   What harder thing then smart, and not to speake?
>   Peace, foolish wit, with wit my wit is mard.
> Thus write I while I doubt to write, and wreake
>   My harmes on Ink's poore losse, perhaps some find
>   *Stella's* great powrs, that so confuse my mind.
>
>   (*AS*, 34)

This is not a very subtle stylistic experiment, but with its enjambments and broken lines it is intended to convey, by contrast with sonnet 1, a heightened sense of confusion in the face of Stella's powers.

Sonnet 35, immediately at its heels, serves as a dramatic answer to the difficulty with words exhibited in 34. It claims a virtue for Astrophel's speechlessness, and the focus shifts to a commentary on the inadequacy of words to praise Stella:

> What may words say, or what may words not say,
>   Where truth it selfe must speake like flatterie?
>   Within what bounds can one his liking stay,
>   Where Nature doth with infinite agree?
> What *Nestor's* counsell can my flames alay,
>   Since Reason's selfe doth blow the cole in me?
>   And ah what hope, that hope should once see day,
>   Where *Cupid* is sworne page to Chastity?
> Honour is honour'd, that thou doest possesse
>   Him as thy slave, and now long needy Fame
>   Doth even grow rich, naming my *Stella's* name.
> Wit learnes in thee perfection to expresse,
>   Not thou by praise, but praise in thee is raisde:
>   It is a praise to praise, when thou art praisde.

(*AS*, 35)

The poem praises Stella through a series of loosely related paradoxes. Its chief interest for us is the introductory wondering question, indicating an uncertainty about the vocabulary of love and its tendency to fall away into mere flattery. The questions of the octet are answered when the poet turns to Stella in the sestet and redefines some of the figures of the earlier part of the sequence. Honor, Fame, and Wit become courtiers in Stella's world, the point of the poem being that love for Stella yokes virtues to their opposites without changing their natures. Honor is "honour'd" by being a slave; Reason "blows the cole"; Wit learns "perfection."

Neither of these sonnets conveys Astrophel's confusion

and wonder at entering Stella's world so well as sonnet 31. This is probably the best known poem of the sequence. It communicates its meaning readily and depends less on context than most of the others. It is worth pointing out, however, the way in which the sonnet combines the traditional melancholy of the lover with the critical wit we have come to associate with Astrophel. In earlier sonnets, "curious wits" have noted his "dull pensivenesse" (sonnet 23) and "darke abstracted guise" (sonnet 27). Sonnet 31 begins with Astrophel in such a pose but sets the courtly figures at a great distance.

> With how sad steps, o Moone, thou climb'st the skies,
>   How silently, and with how wanne a face,
>   What, may it be that even in heav'nly place
>   That busie archer his sharpe arrowes tries?
> Sure, if that long with *Love* acquainted eyes
>   Can judge of *Love*, thou feel'st a Lover's case;
>   I reade it in thy lookes, thy languisht grace,
>   To me that feele the like, thy state descries.
> Then ev'n of fellowship, o Moone, tell me
>   Is constant *Love* deem'd there but want of wit?
>   Are Beauties there as proud as here they be?
> Do they above love to be lov'd, and yet
>   Those Lovers scorne whom that *Love* doth possesse?
>   Do they call *Vertue* there ungratefulnesse?
>
> (*AS*, 31)

The movement of this sonnet is unique; nothing in *Astrophel and Stella* matches it. (Indeed, it is the closest thing in Sidney's sonnets to the pastoral meditations that one finds so frequently in Petrarch's poetry.) For a moment the poet stands outside the press of the courtly world. He finally returns to comment on the "courtly Nymphs," and characteristically the meaning of the sonnet hinges on definitions of terms that haunt the entire sequence: love, virtue, wit. But sharpness, conflict, and satire are muted here in a particularly attractive way.

The octet is concerned with Astrophel's melancholy; his address to the moon gives some measure of his isolation from both Stella and the world around him. The address conveys increasing surprise that even in heaven the lover's long sorrows have a place. He begins in a tone of hushed wonder with the slow moving monosyllables of the opening line, with the lulling repetitions ("how sad . . . / How silently . . . how wanne") and the lovely fall of "silently," the only polysyllable in the two lines. The advance toward "fellowship" with the moon is tentative, moving from the awed exclamations and questions of the first quatrain and the hesitant "What, may it be" of line 3 to the more certain yoking of lines 5–8 ("Sure, if that long with *Love* acquainted eyes").

Having established himself poetically as a true lover, a fellow of the moon in his "languisht grace," he turns the reader's attention back to the courtly world as it might be viewed from the Olympian perspective of his newly affirmed solidarity. The point of the bewildered questions in the sestet is to make the values of Stella and the court beauties seem outlandish. The implication is that, if by fancy the moon could be a lover, surely — although it is itself so changeable — it could not be subject to the irrationalities of these court ladies. In addition to the inevitable burdens of the "Lover's case," Astrophel discovers that his constant love is deemed "want of wit"; that his virtue is called "ungratefulnesse" (by which he must mean it is unpleasing).[16] The sonnet thus takes up an earlier concern: his wit, once an ally of reason, has been converted to the services and praise of Stella (see sonnets 18 and 35); yet she is evidently embarrassed by his attentions and finds them in fact a "want of wit." Virtue, too, clearly means something different to him from what it means to Stella; for her it is a kind of false pride. The clash of definitions creates the delightful mockery of the last line and heralds the long series of dramatic clashes over virtue and love in *Astrophel and Stella*.

Sonnet 31 combines the ingredients of most of Sidney's sonnets in surprisingly different proportions. From one point of view, it is a witty and critical poem involving some of the same mockery of Stella and the court ladies that one finds in sonnet 45. The identification with the moon is in that case a clever tactic to lend cachet to his criticisms. But such a description ignores the main ingredient of the poem: the tone of wonder and frustration with which Astrophel assumes his critical role. Especially in the octet, he conveys a sense of his own awkwardness and separateness without the ferocity and brashness that characterize some of the other sonnets.

Sonnets 38 and 39 are also nocturnal meditations in which Astrophel's critical bent is muted. Sonnet 39 is better known, partly because of its sonorous opening: "Come sleepe, o sleepe, the certaine knot of peace / The baiting place of wit, the balme of woe." The two sonnets provide interesting reading side by side as variations on a theme. (If I consider number 38 in greater detail, it is only because it is a less familiar version of the theme.) The success of these sonnets on sleep depends upon the sense of release they offer. Daniel's "Care-charmer sleep" promises relief from "languish"; "With dark, forgetting of my cares, return." Sleep in Sidney's sonnet 39 becomes "the balme of woe, / The poore man's wealth, the prisoner's release." It shields the lover from despair; above all, it allows him to see the image of his mistress. In a clumsier sonnet, number 32, Morpheus brings Stella to Astrophel in dreams, stealing her image

from his heart. Sonnet 39 presents the vision more grace-
fully, offering her image to the lover as the final temptation
to woo sleep. After "smooth pillowes, sweetest bed, / A
chamber deafe to noise, and blind to light" he promises,
"thou shalt in me / Livelier than else-where *Stella's* image
see."

Sonnet 38, particularizing the process and the ironies of
dreaming of Stella, offers less security in repose:

> This night while sleepe begins with heavy wings
>   To hatch mine eyes, and that unbitted thought
>   Doth fall to stray, and my chiefe powres are brought
>   To leave the scepter of all subject things,
> The first that straight my fancie's error brings
>   Unto my mind, is *Stella's* image, wrought
>   By *Love's* owne selfe, but with so curious drought,
>   That she, me thinks, not onely shines but sings.
> I start, looke, hearke, but what in closde up sence
>   Was held, in opend sense it flies away,
>   Leaving me nought but wailing eloquence:
> I, seeing better sights in sight's decay,
>   Cald it anew, and wooed sleepe againe:
>   But him her host that unkind guest had slaine.
>
> (*AS*, 38)

The sonnet maintains a delicate balance between the
worlds of closed and open sense, between the uncertainties
of the waking world and the joys of sleep. This vision of
Stella is one of the few moments of imagination, untroubled
by desire and affectation, granted to Astrophel in the sequence. Stella's image comes quietly, indeed almost drifts
into the poem. The verbs of the first quatrain give the
sense of process, of progression ("begins . . . / To hatch . . .
/ Doth fall to stray") along with the welcome compulsion
of the passive construction ("are brought / To leave"). With
the heavy grace of sleep comes the release of coltish thought.
What is happening is an abdication of Reason with its hard

bit and scepter, a process accomplished with violence in sonnet 4 ("Thy scepter use in some olde *Catoe's* brest"), but
here performed with dignity and a sense of ceremony: "To
leave the scepter of all subject things." "Fancie's error"
introduces the brilliant vision of Stella, this perfect artifact
wrought by Love — Sidney gives "wrought" special emphasis — with all the strangeness of an image that "not onely
shines but sings."

The brilliance of Stella's image and the harmonies of its
presentation lead inevitably to the broken rhythms of Astrophel's response in the sestet: "I start, looke, hearke." The
vision has been so striking that it cannot be maintained "in
opend sense." Instead of the singing of Stella's image, we are
left with the "wailing eloquence" of Astrophel, and with the
ironies of his wooing sleep rather than the real Stella whom,
in opened sense, he can never see with such clarity. It is
thoroughly in keeping with the tone of *Astrophel and Stella*
that visions of Stella should be fleeting, delicate, and hard
to sustain. We need only think of a related Shakespeare
sonnet, number 27, to understand the characteristic quality
of Sidney's poem:

> Weary with toil, I haste me to my bed,
> The dear repose for limbs with travel tired,
> But then begins a journey in my head
> To work my mind when body's work's expired;
> For then my thoughts, from far where I abide,
> Intend a zealous pilgrimage to thee,
> And keep my drooping eyelids open wide,
> Looking on darkness which the blind do see;
> Save that my soul's imaginary sight
> Presents thy shadow to my sightless view,
> Which, like a jewel hung in ghastly night,
> Makes black night beauteous and her old face new.
>   Lo, thus, by day my limbs, by night my mind,
>   For thee and for myself no quiet find.

Shakespeare also attributes strange powers to his beloved's image, the radiance of "a jewel hung in ghastly night." Furthermore, he leaves us with the impression at the end of the poem that it can glorify and transform "black night." Sidney, on the other hand, qualifies the brilliance of Astrophel's experience almost immediately with his awakening, his sharp reaction, and with the final irony that the vision has now become an "unkind guest," a slayer of the sleep that brought it. He seems almost exaggeratedly concerned with Astrophel's mental process. Sidney must begin with a serious putting aside of reason; in Shakespeare's sonnet, the speaker is merely weary and hastens to a real bed. For Shakespeare's figure, vision comes from the "soul's imaginary sight" rather than from the more ambiguous "fancie's error" of Astrophel. Even in a moment of relaxation, Sidney starts by reminding us of the graver contexts within which a lover's visions may be presented.

5

The poems that follow the vision of sonnets 38 and 39 and lead up to the intense climax in sonnets 69–72 comprise a mixed bag. They are the heart of the entire sequence of 108, but do not hold many surprises for us. Here Sidney comes closer than at any other point in the cycle to a Petrarchan evaluation of Stella; accordingly, these sonnets, though essential to the sequence, are not its most original achievements. The tone is one of fluent supplication:

> O eyes, which do the Spheares of beautie move,
>> Whose beames be joyes, whose joyes all vertues be,
>> Who while they make *Love* conquer, conquer *Love*,
>> The schooles where *Venus* hath learn'd Chastitie.

(AS, 42)

Soule's joy, bend not those morning starres from me,
  Where Vertue is made strong by Beautie's might,
  Where *Love* is chastnesse, Paine doth learne delight,
  And Humblenesse growes one with Majestie.

(*AS*, 48)

These poems provide rare resolutions of virtue and desire.
Along with the smooth praise of Stella, they bring together
Venus and chastity, delight and pain. The Petrarchan contraries we recognize immediately, but still Petrarch's assured
balance is in Sidney's sequence the achievement of a moment, a mood apt to be broken by the intrusion of desire.
Astrophel does not exercise patience, the inescapable virtue
of the Petrarchan lover. Patience becomes in fact one of the
personified virtues that undergoes challenge from Astrophel:

No Patience, if thou wilt my good, then make
  Her come, and heare with patience my desire,
  And then with patience bid me beare my fire.

(*AS*, 56)

Even after the concords of the opening of sonnet 48,
Sidney turns at the end to remind the reader of the destructive power of love:

Yet since my death-wound is already got,
  Deare Killer, spare not they sweet cruell shot:
  A kind of grace it is to slay with speed.

The last line imitates Petrarch,[17] but it is interesting that
Sidney draws upon Petrarch for reminders of Stella's will-
fulness without absorbing the continuing tone of awe that
dominates the *Rime*. The momentary spell that her virtue
has cast upon Astrophel at the outset of the sonnet is broken
by the sly, impatient, and knowing gesture at its close. Three
sonnets earlier, in number 45, Stella's virtue appears to
Astrophel as nothing but a courtly pose: "I am not I, pitie

[1 6 9]

the tale of me." The point to be made about this central
group of sonnets is that, read in sequence, they present a
constantly shifting equilibrium of forces. At some points
(42, 48) Stella's virtue leads convincingly to harmony; at
others it is praised in so flamboyant a fashion as to sound
like parody of the courtly compliment that Sidney criticizes.
In sonnet 44, for example, he excuses Stella for not hearing
his complaints and pitying him:

> The heav'nly nature of that place is such,
> That once come there, the sobs of mine annoyes
> Are metamorphosd straight to tunes of joyes.

What appears to be a firm concord of desire and virtue
in sonnets 42 and 48 seems to be an uneasy alliance in the
light of sonnets like 46, 49, and 52. Young claims that desire
is first acknowledged in sonnet 46. It would be more precise
to say that Astrophel has been conscious of desire throughout the sequence and is now willing to assert it as the irre-
ducible element in his love for Stella. The assertion is made
in a variety of tones, from the serious conflict in sonnet 71,
toward which this group of sonnets builds, to the wicked and
amused assertions of sonnet 52. The latter, a tale of Cupid,
proclaims that "a strife is growne betweene *Vertue* and *Love*."
Each claims Stella for his own, Virtue because it controls
her soul, Cupid because he reigns in her physical beauty.
Astrophel announces himself unabashedly an ally of Cupid,
ridiculing the rigidity of Virtue:

> Well, *Love*, since this demurre our sute doth stay,
> Let *Vertue* have that *Stella's* selfe; yet thus,
> That *Vertue* but that body graunt to us.
>
> (*AS*, 52)

Sonnets 61 and 62 take up the argument with more sense
of an impasse and more respect for Stella's protestations.

Both poems quibble over the definition of love. Of the two, 62 is the better poem:

> Late tyr'd with wo, even ready for to pine
>> With rage of *Love*, I cald my Love unkind;
>> She in whose eyes *Love*, though unfelt, doth shine,
>> Sweet said that I true love in her should find.
> I joyed, but straight thus watred was my wine,
>> That love she did, but loved a Love not blind,
>> Which would not let me, whom she loved, decline
>> From nobler course, fit for my birth and mind:
> And therefore by her Love's authority,
>> Willd me these tempests of vaine love to flie,
>> And anchor fast my selfe on *Vertue's* shore.
> Alas, if this the only mettall be
>> Of *Love*, new-coind to helpe my beggery,
>> Deare, love me not, that you may love me more.
>
> (AS, 62)

Astrophel has been forced in this sonnet to define love quite explicitly as desire. For him it has become increasingly violent, here "rage," as opposed to what Stella calls "true love," "a Love not blind." Her vocabulary belongs to the world of ideal public behavior from which he has already fallen; her love is identified with the "nobler course, fit for my birth and mind." Stella's rhetoric is formal: she identifies his love with the conventional lover's "tempests." But all the energy of the sonnet comes from Astrophel's speech, with his rage, his joy, and, above all, his colloquialisms: "thus watred was my wine." He labels Stella's exhortations as a willful coining of argument (line 13). He delights in his critical role, in his "beggery," and the technique we have noted as characteristic of the sequence, the discovery of conflict by the plain-speaker, is finally used to acknowledge his "Love" for what it is. Astrophel has repeated the process of the opening sonnets, a fall from grace — here from the virtue of love, earlier from the virtue of public life — and in the process discovered the source of his own critical energy.

Astrophel and Stella reaches a climax in sonnets 69–72. We have already examined number 71 in detail, but it is illuminating to come upon it in the context of the sequence. There we see how it gains and imparts meaning as one of a cluster of sonnets that mark a turning point in the implied action of the cycle. Sidney begins in sonnet 69 with a series of exclamations, at least one to each line of the octet. Not until the sestet does he give the reason for Astrophel's happiness:

> For *Stella* hath with words where faith doth shine,
>   Of her high heart giv'n me the monarchie:
> I, I, o I may say, that she is mine.
> And though she give but thus conditionly
>   This realme of blisse, while vertuous course I take,
>   No kings be crown'd but they some covenants make.
>
> (AS, 69)

The poem, for all its enthusiasm, is not without its irony. According to the last tercet, Astrophel plans to turn a limited into an absolute monarchy; both the imagery and excited tone seem to indicate that Astrophel is overlooking Stella's "conditionly" in his delight at receiving power. The effect is reinforced by the aphoristic and dismissive closing line of the poem; Stella's stipulation that he maintain a "vertuous course" occurs almost as an afterthought, and the implication of his final statement is that covenants must be made — and broken — by the experienced *politique*.

In the midst of this section on what appears to be achieved love comes sonnet 70, marking the appearance of the verses on poetry that recur at crucial moments in the sequence. Here the urgencies of sonnet 69 transform themselves into a declared independence of the public standards of lament:

"Sonets be not bound prentise to annoy: / Trebles sing high, as well as bases deepe." The exultation is somewhat qualified by the poem's conclusion:

> Cease eager Muse, peace pen, for my sake stay,
>   I give you here my hand for truth of this,
>   Wise silence is best musicke unto blisse.   (*AS*, 70)

The final line is one of Sidney's loveliest; without destroying the mood, it adds a sobering note in the opening "Wise." The weight of Sidney's line can be appreciated by comparison with its equally felicitous Shakespearean cousin: "Silence is the perfectest herald of joy." [18] Both lines carry a hushed expectation of love; in Sidney's there is also an incipient warning against hubris.

After the abandonment of complaint in sonnets 69 and 70, Sidney turns his energy toward testing his "blisse," only to discover once again his passionate difference from Stella: "'But ah,' Desire still cries, 'give me some food.'" He has now evaluated Stella's "condition" of sonnet 69, and sonnet 72 completes the movement. The loyalties it weighs are those of 71, but the tone is noticeably different:

> Desire, though thou my old companion art,
>   And oft so clings to my pure Love, that I
>   One from the other scarcely can descrie,
>   While each doth blow the fier of my hart;
> Now from thy fellowship I needs must part,
>   *Venus* is taught with *Dian's* wings to flie:
>   I must no more in thy sweet passions lie:
>   *Vertue's* gold now must head my *Cupid's* dart.
> Service and Honor, wonder with delight,
>   Feare to offend, will worthie to appeare,
>   Care shining in mine eyes, faith in my sprite,
> These things are left me by my only Deare;
>   But thou Desire, because thou wouldst have all,
>   Now banisht art, but yet alas how shall?   (*AS*, 72)

In a sequence filled with adversaries, Astrophel recognizes Desire as a companion. The attractions of "pure love" and "Vertue's gold" are expressed with as much grace as they are in sonnet 71; but Desire is not a harsh intruder who enters the poem at its close, as he does in the preceding sonnet. He is the tried friend, the oldest loyalty. Sidney has organized the poem with dramatic skill, particularly in the tone of voice with which he addresses the personified Desire — the reluctance with which Desire is banished and the puzzlement and quiet resignation with which he is retained at the close.

Within the space of four sonnets, Sidney has described an arc of emotion that reproduces the sequence in small: Astrophel began with delight in love and ends by acknowledging his inevitable separation from Stella, a separation enforced by the strength of his desire. The four sonnets demonstrate the relative freedom with which Sidney interlaces Astrophel's private responses to love and the values of the Petrarchan convention. The energy displayed in sonnets 69 and 70 is immediately qualified when judged against Stella's perfection in 71. "No kings be crown'd but they some covenants make" at the end of 69 must be reinterpreted, in the light of the convention, as an assertion of desire, a reminder of the kind of compromise demanded by love. Then the convention itself is questioned as Astrophel's long-standing attachment to desire is dramatized, in sonnet 72, as a force to be reckoned with. The continued shifting of position, the continued revaluation of Astrophel's experience from various points of view, is something that Sidney can accomplish in a sequence. Because his sonnets do not rely upon the multiple meanings of individual lines or upon metaphorical complication in their verbs and adjectives, the degree of suggestiveness of any single sonnet is limited. But some sonnets fall into natural groups. Each sonnet of the group 69–72 makes in its final line a simple alteration of the assumptions about love or love poetry with which that particular sonnet began. Viewed altogether they provide an interesting range of responses to Astrophel's newly found felicity.

6

After sonnet 72, the references to a narrative background in the sequence increase. One of the difficulties in deciding just what series of events lies behind the poems stems from the fact that one cannot be certain what place is occupied by the eleven songs, clearly meant to be part of *Astrophel and Stella*. These songs carry a heavy narrative burden. Though printed at the close of the series in the two quartos issued by Thomas Newman, they were set into the text in the more reliable version of *Astrophel and Stella* included in the 1598 folio that was prepared under the supervision of the Countess of Pembroke. There is every dramatic justification for the latter arrangement. Six of the eleven songs are clustered between sonnets 85 and 87, and those songs provide a necessary narrative bridge between an anticipated meeting with Stella (85) and what appears to be a separation enforced by "iron lawes of duty" (87). After that point, the sonnets continually lament the separation of the lovers.

The songs and sonnets after number 72 act within the framework carefully prepared before and climaxed in sonnets 69–72. Most in this later group are concerned with Astrophel's pressing his desires against Stella's injunctions to virtue. The songs actually bring Stella on stage, presenting her as a speaker, and they particularize the conflict that the rest of the cycle has made abundantly clear. Several of the sonnets are *baisers*, flamboyant inventions on the theme of Stella's kiss. One sample will indicate the tone: "Sweet swelling lip, well maist thou swell in pride, / Since best wits thinke it wit thee to admire" (*AS*, 80). These poems, as Janet Scott has pointed out,[19] are based, significantly, not upon Petrarch but upon a later vogue in Italian and French sonnets. They convey elegant suggestion and Cavalier invitation, tones generally absent from Petrarch's *Rime*.[20] Desire is allowed to pass with fewer challenges from Petrarchans and Platonists. The section before sonnet 87 allows a moment of sensual relaxation in *Astrophel and Stella*. The songs introduce pastoral *otium*, which has not been permitted in the earlier sonnets:

> In a grove most rich of shade,
> Where birds wanton musicke made,
> May then yong his pide weedes showing,
> New perfumed with flowers fresh growing,
>
> *Astrophel* with *Stella* sweete,
> Did for mutuall comfort meete.
>
> (*AS*, eighth song)

The promise of spring in sonnets 69 and 70 is realized ("Gone is the winter of my miserie" [69]; "Griefe but *Love's* winter liverie is" [70]). The fourth song invites Stella to pastoral pleasures:

> These sweet flowers on fine bed too,
> Us in their best language woo:
> Take me to thee, and thee to me.
> 'No, no, no, no, my Deare, let be.'

In the third song Astrophel praises her in language that realizes the fleeting dream of sonnet 38: she "not onely shines but sings."

> If *Orpheus'* voyce had force to breathe such musicke's love
> Through pores of senceless trees, as it could make them move:
> If stones good measure daunc'd, the Theban walles to build,
> To cadence of the tunes, which *Amphyon's* lyre did yeeld,

More cause a like effect at leastwise bringeth:
O stones, o trees, learne hearing, *Stella* singeth.

. . . . .

If Eagle fierce could so in *Grecian* Mayd delight,
As his light was her eyes, her death his endlesse night:
Earth gave that Love, heav'n I trow Love refineth:
O birds, o beasts, looke Love, lo, *Stella* shineth.

Such concentration of harmonies in the sequence is astonishing and short-lived. It is significant that pastoral richness and fulfillment recur throughout Petrarch's cycle and
throughout Spenser's, but represent only a momentary lyric
grace in *Astrophel and Stella*. As one would expect from the
movement of the sequence, Astrophel's desire blights the
promise of concord in love; he is forced, in sonnet 87, to
leave Stella forever.

The final sonnets of the cycle perform a ceremony of grief.
Astrophel addresses the personified companions of his woe:
Grief (94), Sighs (95), Thought (96), Tears (100), Absence
(106), Sorrow (108). I cannot agree with Young that Sidney,
in his grief, at last finds meaning in Petrarchan conventions.[21] The vision of Laura that comes to Petrarch in her
absence and after her death causes him pain, but it also has
power to sustain him. For the unrelieved sorrow of the last
poems of *Astrophel and Stella*, there is much less consolation. Just as the fierceness of thwarted desire lies behind the
inconsolable grief of the double sestina in the *Arcadia*, so
here that force lends a special ferocity to Sidney's imagery:

While the blacke horrors of the silent night,
Paint woe's blacke face so lively to my sight,
That tedious leasure marks each wrinckled line:
But when *Aurora* leades out *Phoebus'* daunce,
Mine eyes then only winke, for spite perchance,
That wormes should have their Sun, and I want mine.

(*AS*, 98)

The same bitterness is present in the poem about sleep and wakefulness that follows (sonnet 99). Again there is no relief for Astrophel's divorce from nature:

> But when birds charme, and that sweet aire, which is
> Morne's messenger, with rose enameld skies
> Cals each wight to salute the floure of blisse;
> In tombe of lids then buried are mine eyes,
> Forst by their Lord, who is asham'd to find
> Such light in sense, with such a darkned mind.

The closing sonnets of the cycle are powerful in their gestures, though not always very successful in their execution. Sidney does not develop a ceremony for grief as successfully in these poems as he did in the double sestina. In fact, the cycle comes to no fitting conclusion; it merely ends. The only possible dramatic resolution for *Astrophel and Stella* comes in two sonnets long printed as part of the sequence, but now divorced from it by critical consent since there is no sixteenth-century precedent for their inclusion. For a poet so pessimistic about desire and about the possible refining power of love, there is real relief in the finality and assurance of the two poems printed for the first time among *Certaine Sonets* appended to the folio of 1598: "Thou blind man's marke, thou foole's selfe chosen snare" and "Leave me o Love, which reachest but to dust." The poems return to Sidney's first definition of virtue, to a guarantee of repose that he cannot find in love:

> For vertue hath this better lesson taught,
> Within my selfe to seeke my onelie hire:
> Desiring nought but how to kill desire.

CONCLUSION

Astrophel and Stella continues Sidney's concern with conflict — the conflict between love and heroic obligation, between desire and virtuous affection. These themes are present, of course, in the *Arcadia*, where love, with all its enriching power, also represents a fall from the world of heroic activity. Sidney's presentation of love is qualified by a memory of innocence and wholeness, a coexistence of action and contemplation, which is reflected in the ardent reasonableness of his heroes. The forester in *The Lady of May* symbolizes that felicitous union. His life combines "countrey quietnesse" and "gallant . . . activity," which strengthen both body and mind. His emblem is the forest around him: "O sweet contentation to see the long life of the hurtlesse trees, to see how in streight growing up, though never so high, they hinder not their fellowes, they enviously trouble, which are crookedly bent." So too Philisides in the *Arcadia*, before he falls in love, enjoys in Samothea an Eden of the mind — an experience Renato Poggioli has termed the "pastoral of the self":

> . . . and there my calmie thoughts I fedd
> On Nature's sweet repast, as healthfull senses ledd.
> Her giftes my study was, her beauties were my sporte:
> My worke her workes to know, her dwelling my resorte.
>
> (*Arc.* 73)

When love enters the pastoral world, that world ceases to resemble Eden and becomes chaotic, a world of comic mistakes and tragic insights. Were it not for some convenient accidents at the close of the *Arcadia*, fulfillment and wholeness in love would lie forever beyond the reach of Pyrocles and Musidorus.

Sidney's achievement in *Astrophel and Stella* is to fashion the Petrarchan sonnet into a form responsive to the antagonisms he felt so deeply. These poems stand in sharp contrast to the simpler verse of the *Arcadia*, whose chief strength lies in its ability to register and amplify a single emotion. In Astrophel, the complex, questioning hero in love, Sidney found an excellent persona; for Astrophel has no one stance, but moves flexibly among a number of changing attitudes. Only momentarily can he entertain the Petrarchan vision of earthly beauty that restores the lover to grace or wisdom. His significant activity is the discovery of conflict, and he delights in it.

Sidney's excessive consciousness of style — his need to write about it, to draw attention to it — indicates that much of the energy of the Italian style had deserted the convention. His sonnets, indeed, signify a discontent with a philosophical and poetic framework that in England, France, and Italy had begun to break down. We need only think of Tasso's complaints against "tyrant honor" in the *Aminta* to understand how debased and attenuated Petrarchan "virtue" had become in the society that Tasso is criticizing. The inevitable decay of a poetic idea, excessively imitated, had taken place. What had begun as an ideal of conduct had ended as an imperative of courtly affectation.

It is important to observe that, while Sidney can point up the inadequacies of the Petrarchan mode, he has no private mode to substitute for it. *Astrophel and Stella* may be considered as a prologue to the satiric examination of the conventions of love poetry that takes place in Shakespeare's major comedies, particularly in *Love's Labour's Lost, Much Ado About Nothing,* and *As You Like It.* The sonnets are closest, however, to *Troilus and Cressida.* Chaucer's Troilus may have been one of Astrophel's "cordialls," but in spirit Astrophel is more like Shakespeare's Troilus, fearfully vexed by desires and confused by the never-relenting demands of the senses. There is a cutting, sardonic edge to Sidney's presentation of Astrophel that is not to be found in Chaucer's delicate and witty portrayal of his courtly lover. Astrophel never resolves the conflict between his own desire and the expectations of wonder that are embodied in the Petrarchan convention. He sees no need to go beyond the acceptance of desire as an emblem of his fall, a source of both disruptive power and vitality, the origin of perpetual conflict.

Sidney's sonnets, in the last analysis, do not dramatize the richness of love that is always present in the imagination of the lover in Petrarch. For a sense of love's renewing power, one turns to the less exciting but more optimistic sonnets of Spenser or to the more complex love poetry of Shakespeare and Donne. But if Sidney is more angular, less inclusive, than those who followed him in English poetry, he is, on the other hand, engaged in an activity that Shakespeare and Donne were to continue. These poets transformed the vocabulary of love poetry in England, though they took very different ways. The author of *Astrophel and Stella* must have represented a liberating force to both of them; for his sonnet sequence raises explicitly the question of the fate of Petrarchism in England and poses more problems about Neoplatonic love in English poetry than it answers.

NOTES

INDEX

NOTES

INTRODUCTION

1. *Orlando Furioso,* tr. Sir John Harington (London: Richard Field, 1591), sig. L4v.

2. William Empson, *Seven Types of Ambiguity* (New York, 1931), pp. 45–50; Theodore Spencer, "The Poetry of Sir Philip Sidney," *ELH,* XII (1945), 264–266.

1. THE TRANSFORMATION OF ARCADIA

1. Erwin Panofsky, "*Et in Arcadia Ego*: Poussin and the Elegiac Tradition," *Meaning in the Visual Arts* (New York: Doubleday Anchor Books, 1955), p. 299.

2. *Ibid.,* p. 303.

3. For Raphael's Parnassus, see G. I. Hoogewerff, "La Stanza della Segnatura," *Rendiconti della Pontificia Accademia Romana di Archeologia,* XXIII–XXIV (1949), 322–334. (I am indebted for this information to Mrs. Angelica Rudenstine.)

For commentaries on Sannazaro's work, see *Arcadia di Jacobo Sannazaro,* ed. Michele Scherillo (Turin, 1888), p. ccxxxv. This edition contains the most complete scholarly introduction to the *Arcadia.* Hereafter cited as Scherillo.

4. Attilio Momigliano, "Jacopo Sannazaro," *Studi di poesia* (Bari, 1948), p. 43. (Bembo's lines are: "De sacro cineri flores, hic ille Maroni / Sincerus Musa proximus ut tumulo." Sincero [Sincerus] is the central figure of Sannazaro's *Arcadia.*) Cervantes, *Viaje al Parnaso,* ch. 3.

5. *The Complete Works of Sir Philip Sidney,* ed. Albert Feuillerat, 4 vols. (Cambridge, Eng., 1912–1926), III, 37. Hereafter cited as *F.*

6. Alice Hulubei, *L'Eglogue en France au XVIe siècle* (Paris, 1938), pp. 6–7; quoted from *L'Arcadie de Messire Jaques Sannazar* (Paris, 1544).

7. Scherillo, p. xxxi.

8. Ernst Robert Curtius, *European Literature and the Latin Middle Ages,* tr. Willard Trask (New York, 1953), p. 187.

9. Jacopo Sannazaro, *Opere,* ed. Enrico Carrara (Turin, 1952), p. 217. Hereafter cited as *Opere.* All quotations from the *Arcadia* are from this modern edition.

10. Virgil, *Eclogues,* I.5. Hereafter cited as *Ecl.*

11. *Opere,* p. 217.

12. Petronius, *Satyricon,* 131.

13. Curtius, p. 195.

14. This eclogue represents one extreme in the Italian *Arcadia*: the sacrifice of poetic content to ingenious form. After an introductory section that involves three changes in meter and rhyme scheme, the contest proper is conducted in (1) *barzelletta,* a form in which the last line of a stanza is repeated as the first line of the following stanza; (2) four madrigal stanzas; (3) sets of *terzine,* which alternate from line to line between the *sdrucciola* and the *piana,* triple and double rhymes.

15. Sannazaro's lines echo precisely Virgil's "maioresque cadunt altis de montibus umbrae." The shepherds in both passages promise simple and satisfying pastoral fare: bread and wine in Sannazaro; ripe apples, chestnuts, and cheese in Virgil.

16. Curtius, p. 195.

17. Scherillo, pp. 6–8. The notes supply sources in great detail.

18. His model is the stanza of Petrarch's "Se'l pensier che mi strugge": abC, abC; cdeeDff.

19. Scherillo, p. 51n. "Sospiro" and "adiro" occur together in Petrarch, *Rime,* 135.

20. *Ecl.* IV.29–30: "incultisque rubens pendebit sentibus uva / et durae quercus sudabunt roscida mella" (on wild brambles shall hang the purple grape, and the stubborn oak shall distil dewy honey).

21. See Petrarch, *Rime,* 293:2: "le voci de' sospir miei in rima."

22. *Rime,* 332:39.

23. See *Opere,* pp. 94–95, ll. 35–39. Here, in the fifth eclogue, he laments the death of Androgeo and pays tribute to his poetic powers.

2. HEROIC AND PASTORAL

1. John Milton, *Eikonoklastes,* ch. 1. Quoted from *The Student's Milton,* ed. Frank Allen Patterson, rev. ed. (New York, 1946), p. 783.

2. *Elizabethan Critical Essays,* ed. G. Gregory Smith (Oxford, 1904), II, 209.

3. Unless specifically noted, all references to *The Countesse of Pembroke's Arcadia* come from the revised version of 1590 and the original version of the last two books added to complete the text in 1593. Feuillerat reprints these five books in the first two volumes of his

edition. The unrevised or original *Arcadia* was not printed until 1926, when it appeared as volume four of the Feuillerat edition.

4. *Elizabethan Critical Essays*, II, 264.

5. Fulke Greville, *Life of Sir Philip Sidney*, ed. Nowell Smith (Oxford, 1907), p. 16.

6. *Arcadia*, No. 4. All quotations of verse from the *Arcadia* are from *The Poems of Sir Philip Sidney*, ed. William A. Ringler, Jr. (Oxford, 1962). Hereafter cited as *Arc.* with the number of the poem in Ringler's edition; the second set of numbers, when given, refers to lines.

7. Ringler, pp. 361–362, suggests May 1579 as an alternative, but prefers the earlier dating. The title, *The Lady of May, a Masque*, was added by the editor of the collection of Sidney's work that appeared in London in 1725.

8. For an excellent discussion of the formal elements of this masque and its innovations, see Stephen Orgel, *The Jonsonian Masque* (Cambridge, Mass., 1965), pp. 44–57.

9. For Espilus as "true pastoralist," see Frank Kermode, ed., *English Pastoral Poetry from the Beginnings to Marvell* (London, 1952), p. 244. This opinion seems peculiar in an otherwise careful set of commentaries.

10. The masque may have some as yet unexplained political reference. Ringler (p. 362) rejects the notion that it refers to the French marriage, which Elizabeth had begun to reconsider in 1578. He suggests a possible reference to Leicester's effort at open aid to continental Protestants by providing military support for the Netherlands.

11. Edmund Spenser, *The Faerie Queene*, VI.x.2–3. All quotations are from *Spenser's Faerie Queene*, ed. J. C. Smith, 2 vols. (Oxford, 1909).

3. THE ARCADIAN RHETORIC

1. The quoted phrase is Gabriel Harvey's, from *Marginalia*, ed. G. C. Moore Smith (Stratford-upon-Avon: Shakespeare Head Press, 1913), p. 226.

2. A theatrical analogy is relevant since, in the unrevised *Arcadia*, the five books are actually referred to as "actes" and the eclogues treated as theatrical interludes or entertainments. The division between eclogues to be read and eclogues to be performed was not a very firm one in the sixteenth century. One of the sources of Italian pastoral drama was the recited eclogue, the *ecloga rappresentativa*, of which an early example is Castiglione's *Tirsi* performed by Castiglione himself with Cesare Gonzaga in 1506. The term eclogue was used as late as 1572 by critics to describe Tasso's *Aminta*, very definitely a theatrical production. See W. W. Greg, *Pastoral Poetry and Pastoral Drama*

(London, 1906), pp. 177ff for *Aminta,* and *passim* for an account of the relation of Italian pastoral poetry to pastoral drama.

3. It is noteworthy that the experiments occur primarily in the eclogues, while the poems in the body of the romance are sonnets or variants of the sonnet form. This is not a rigid practice, however, since in the revised version, many of the experimental eclogues are shifted into the body of the romance.

4. Ringler, *Poems,* p. xxxiv.

5. For a detailed analysis of the meter of this poem, see Theodore Spencer, "The Poetry of Sir Philip Sidney," *ELH,* XII (1945), 262–263. The eclogue moves in *terzine* from sections in triple rhyme to feminine endings and finally masculine rhymes. It continues with *frottola* and a *barzelletta,* both used in the Sannazaro poem.

6. This poem is not in the 1590 *Arcadia* but does appear in the folio of 1593.

7. *Arc.* 63. The work resembles Spenser's "Epithalamion" in some ways, particularly in its orderly progression by stanzas with refrain, each stanza introducing new tributes from Muses, Earth, Nymphs, etc. Characteristically, half of Sidney's poem is devoted to banishing possible dangers of love, particularly jealousy and "foule Cupid, syre to lawlesse lust."

8. In another poem (*Arc.* 72) Strephon and Klaius introduce the emblem of fishing for the "fish Torpedo faire" as equivalent to the lover's experience. "The catcher now is caught," lamed by his own desires.

9. Empson, *Seven Types of Ambiguity* (New York, 1931), pp. 45ff.

10. *Ibid.,* p. 48.

11. Spencer, p. 265.

12. Empson, p. 50. "Flatly" is Empson's revision of 1947. The 1931 edition, which I cite throughout, reads "patiently."

13. Roman Jakobson, "Poetry of Grammar and Grammar of Poetry," *Poetics,* Polska Akademia NAUK, Instytut Badan Literackich (Warsaw, 1961). Unpublished illustrations to this paper include a discussion of Sidney, *Arc.* 20.

14. Abraham Fraunce, *The Arcadian Rhetorike,* ed. Ethel Seaton (Oxford, 1950), p. 53.

15. George Puttenham terms such figures "sententious," in *The Arte of English Poesie,* ed. Gladys D. Willcock and Alice Walker (Cambridge, Eng., 1936), p. 196. Fraunce distinguishes "figures" — repeated patterns in several words — from "tropes" or "turnings" of single words from their "naturall signification" (p. 3). In the latter category are such devices as metaphor and synecdoche; in the former, such rhetorical patterns as anaphora, anadiplosis, and epistrophe.

16. See Robert L. Montgomery, *Symmetry and Sense*: *The Poetry of Sir Philip Sidney* (Austin, 1961).

17. This conceit is a congenial one for Sidney. See *Certaine Sonets*, 3.

18. Fraunce, pp. 36–37; "*Anadiplosis*, redubling, or reduplication is when the same sound is repeated in the ende of the sentence going before, and in the beginning of the sentence following after."

19. Quoted from *Tottel's Miscellany*, ed. Hyder Rollins (Cambridge, Mass., 1928), I, 9.

20. *Ibid.*, I, 10–11.

21. *Arc.* 47. The sonnet "Do not disdaine" is the first in the book to divide the sestet into tercets in its rhyme scheme.

22. See *Arc.* 60, for instance. The sonnet experiments with handling three subjects and three verbs simultaneously.

23. The principal relationships are: Plexirtus is the half-brother of Andromana; her husband is the uncle of Artaxia, who marries Plexirtus.

24. See Hallett Smith, *Elizabethan Poetry: A Study in Conventions, Meaning, and Expression* (Cambridge, Mass., 1952), p. 11.

4. THE PETRARCHAN VISION

1. There were three unauthorized quartos of the sequence (two in 1591, printed by Thomas Newman, and one printed by Matthew Lownes, probably 1597–1600), in addition to the canonical version of the sonnets included by the Countess of Pembroke in her folio edition of the *Arcadia*, 1598. See Ringler's description of manuscripts and early editions in *Poems*, pp. 538–546.

2. The most recent and most intelligent discussion of this problem is that of Jack Stillinger, "The Biographical Problem of *Astrophel and Stella*," *Journal of English and Germanic Philology*, LIX (1960), 617–639.

3. Critical attention to the poetic problems in *Astrophel and Stella* has increased since Theodore Spencer's 1945 article on Sidney's poetry. See also Ringler's introduction and notes in *Poems*; Robert L. Montgomery, *Symmetry and Sense* (Austin, 1961); and Hallett Smith, *Elizabethan Poetry* (Cambridge, Mass., 1952), pp. 142–158. Also J. W. Lever, *The Elizabethan Love Sonnet* (London, 1956), pp. 51–91, and Richard B. Young, "English Petrarke: A Study of Sidney's *Astrophel and Stella*," in *Three Studies in the Renaissance: Sidney, Jonson, Milton* (New Haven, 1958), pp. 1–88.

4. *Astrophel and Stella*, No. 15. All quotations are from Ringler, *Poems*, hereafter cited *AS* followed by the number of the sonnet in Ringler's edition.

5. Sidney's own reaction to Ciceronianism is interesting in the light of the critique of Petrarch's unquestioning imitators implied in *Astrophel and Stella*. He wrote to his brother Robert: "So you can speak and write Latin, not barbarously, I never require great study in Ciceronianism, the chief abuse of Oxford, *Qui dum verba sectantur, res ipsas negligunt.*" The letter is dated 18 October 1580 and is quoted in M. W. Wallace, *The Life of Sir Philip Sidney* (Cambridge, Eng., 1915), p. 225.

6. A notable and surprising exception is the sestina, "A qualunque animale alberga in terra," *Rime*, No. 22.

7. Adelia Noferi, "Per una storia dello stile Petrarchesco," *Poesia*, V (1946), 10.

8. Virgil, *Aeneid*, I.319–320. An interesting poetic transfer, conscious or unconscious, has taken place. The Latin *nodo*, which refers to Venus' garment, becomes the Italian *nodi*, used to describe Laura's hair twisted by the wind.

9. For a discussion of the power of *memoria* in the *Rime*, see Noferi, pp. 15ff.

10. Horace, *Odes*, I.xxii.23–24.

11. Petrarch, *Familiari*, II.ix. Translation by Theodor Mommsen in Petrarch, *Songs and Sonnets* (New York, 1946), p. xxxiii.

12. Young, p. 88.

13. Janet G. Scott, *Les Sonnets elisabéthains* (Paris, 1929), p. 306, points out this connection. See also Lever, pp. 58–62.

14. Baldessare Castiglione, *The Book of the Courtier*, tr. Hoby, The Tudor Translations (London, 1900), p. 363.

15. Sixty sonnets in *Astrophel and Stella* follow this form exactly. The octave ABBA/ABBA, in combination with the regular sestet or some other arrangement, is used seventy-five times. Sidney's regular sestet CDC/DEE, combined with the octave ABBA/ABBA or in some other arrangement, appears in eighty-five sonnets.

16. Rosemond Tuve, *Elizabethan and Metaphysical Imagery* (Chicago, 1947), p. 39.

17. *Elizabethan Critical Essays*, ed. G. Gregory Smith (Oxford, 1904), I, 48.

18. For an extended discussion, see Lisle C. John, *The Elizabethan Sonnet Sequences* (New York, 1938), pp. 56ff.

19. Lines 1–4 appear as an example of the rhetorical figure "climax" in Fraunce's *The Arcadian Rhetorike*. "*Climax*, gradation, is a reduplication continued by divers degrees and steps, as it were, of the same word or sound." See *The Arcadian Rhetorike*, ed. Ethel Seaton (Oxford, 1950), pp. 38–39.

20. See Arthur Dickson, "Sidney's *Astrophel and Stella*, Sonnet I," *The Explicator*, III, no. 1 (1944).

21. Thomas Wilson, *The Arte of Rhetorique* (1560), ed. G. H. Mair (Oxford, 1909), p. 5. One finds the figure also in E. K.'s prefatory remarks to *The Shepheardes Calendar*. The original source appears to be Cicero, *De oratore*, II.xiv.60. It is of course part of the wit of the poem that Sidney should use the learned reference against the excesses of learning.

22. For a discussion of Renaissance uses of "invention," see Tuve, pp. 310ff.

23. For an interesting discussion of this point from another angle, see Young, p. 8.

24. See Smith, pp. 142–157, which discusses the contradiction in terms of the two audiences, the lady and the reader, to whom the sequence is directed.

25. *Ibid.*, p. 149.

5. THE SEQUENCE

1. Thomas Nashe, "Somewhat to read for them that list" — prefaced to Newman's first quarto of *Astrophel and Stella,* 1591. Quoted from *F,* III.370.

2. Harvey, *Marginalia,* ed. Smith, p. 228.

3. Charles Lamb, "Some Sonnets of Sir Philip Sydney," *The Works of Charles and Mary Lamb,* ed. E. V. Lucas, 7 vols. (New York, 1903), II, 218.

4. *Ibid.*

5. For an interesting discussion of this theme, see Robert L. Montgomery, *Symmetry and Sense* (Austin, 1961), ch. 5.

6. Richard B. Young, "English Petrarke," in *Three Studies in the Renaissance: Sidney, Jonson, Milton* (New Haven, 1958), p. 31.

7. Lisle C. John, *The Elizabethan Sonnet Sequences* (New York, 1938), p. 67.

8. Cf. *The Merchant of Venice,* III.ii.63–71: "Tell me where is fancy bred, / Or in the heart or in the head? / . . . It is engend'red in the eyes, / With gazing fed."

9. See Ringler's note, *Poems,* p. 469.

10. L. G. Salingar, "The Elizabethan Literary Renaissance," *The Age of Shakespeare,* Pelican Guide to English Literature, II (London, 1955), 94.

11. C. S. Lewis, *English Literature in the Sixteenth Century* (Oxford, 1954), p. 372.

12. Edmund Spenser, *Amoretti,* No. 79. Quoted from *The Poetical Works of Edmund Spenser,* ed. Smith and De Selincourt (Oxford, 1912).

13. Tuve, p. 321.

14. Young, p. 50.

15. *Ibid.*, pp. 51–52.

16. There is understandable confusion over the proper reading of the last line. Lamb believes the line to be inverted and that Astrophel means to say that among the ladies Stella's "ungratefulnesse" is called "Vertue." In this case "ungrateful" would carry its modern meaning of "lacking in gratitude" (to Astrophel for loving her). I have preferred the contrary reading in order to avoid reversing the word order in what seems an awkward fashion, and also because the quibble over the definition of virtue seems more in tune with Sidney's concerns in the sonnet than a quibble over the definition of ungratefulness.

17. "Un modo di pietate, occider tosto." *Rime*, 207, line 88. See also Janet G. Scott, *Les Sonnets elisabéthains* (Paris, 1929), p. 305.

18. Shakespeare, *Much Ado About Nothing*, II.i.317.

19. Scott, pp. 27–29.

20. For one example, see *AS*, 76, which parallels Stella's arrival with the appearance of the sun. It closes: "No wind, no shade can coole, what helpe then in my case, / But with short breath, long lookes, staid feet and walking hed, / Pray that my sunne go downe with meeker beames to bed."

21. Young, p. 88.

INDEX

[193]

BRITISH LITERATURE IN
NORTON PAPERBOUND EDITIONS

THE NORTON LIBRARY

Jane Austen *Persuasion* (N163)

Robert Browning *The Ring and the Book* (N433)

Anthony Burgess *A Clockwork Orange* (N224)
Tremor of Intent (N416)

Fanny Burney *Evelina* (N294)

Joseph Conrad *The Arrow of Gold* (N458)
Chance (N456)
The Rescue (N457)

Maria Edgeworth *Castle Rackrent* (N288)

Henry Fielding *Joseph Andrews* (N274)

Mrs. Gaskell *Mary Barton* (N245)

Edmund Gosse *Father and Son* (N195)

Henry Mackenzie *The Man of Feeling* (N214)

Thomas Love Peacock *Nightmare Abbey* (N283)

Samuel Richardson *Pamela* (N166)

Anthony Trollope *The Last Chronicle of Barset* (N291)

NORTON CRITICAL EDITIONS

Jane Austen *Pride and Prejudice* (Donald Gray, ed.)

Emily Brontë *Wuthering Heights* (William M. Sale, Jr., ed.)

Joseph Conrad *Heart of Darkness* (Robert Kimbrough, ed.)
Lord Jim (Thomas Moser, ed.)

Charles Dickens *Hard Times* (George Ford and Sylvère Monod, eds.)

John Donne *John Donne's Poetry* (A. L. Clements, ed.)

Thomas Hardy *Tess of the D'Urbervilles* (Scott Elledge, ed.)

John Henry Cardinal Newman *Apologia Pro Vita Sua* (David DeLaura, ed.)

William Shakespeare *Hamlet* (Cyrus Hoy, ed.)
Henry IV, Part I (James L. Sanderson, ed.)

Jonathan Swift *Gulliver's Travels* (Robert A. Greenberg, ed.)